# AFRICAN TWILIGHT

## THE STORY OF A HUNTER

## Robert F. Jones

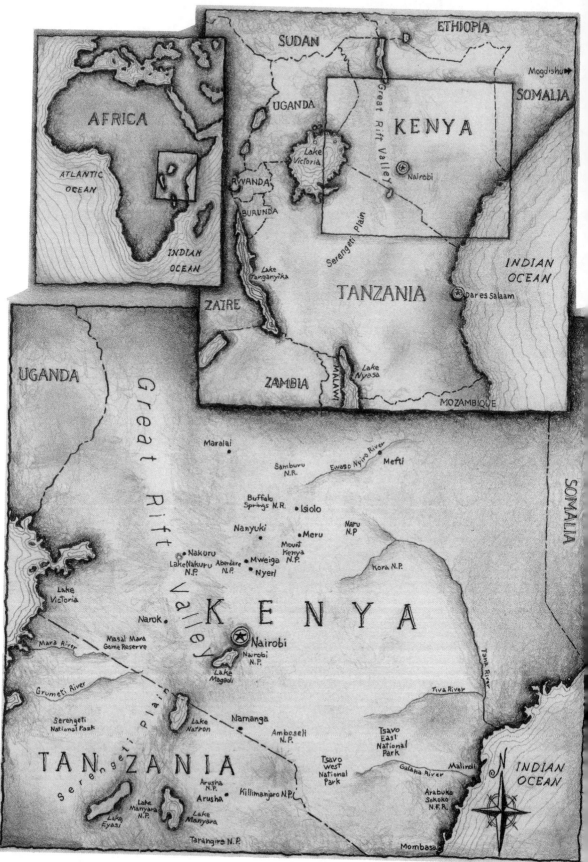

Illustration by Joseph R. McGurn

# AfricaN
## TWILIGHT

### The Story of a Hunter

### Robert F. Jones

Published by Wilderness Adventures Press™
P.O. Box 1410
Bozeman, MT 59771

10 9 8 7 6 5 4 3 2 1

Printed in the United States of America

ISBN 1-885106-09-2
Limited Edition of 375 ISBN    1-885106-10-6

"...the sparkling torrential rains, the sweeping thunderstorms, the grass fires creeping over the veld at night like snakes of living flame, the glorious aspect of the heavens, now of a spotless blue, now charged with the splendid and many-coloured lights of sunset, and now sparkling with a myriad stars, the wine-like taste of the air upon the plains, the beautiful flowers in the bush-clad *kloofs*—all these things impressed me, so much that were I to live a thousand years I never should forget them."

—H. Rider Haggard, 1925

**For John Holt & Steve Bodio—who should have been there...**

# Contents

# Preface
## *Moyo Ni Moja*

I LOVE TO HUNT, ESPECIALLY IN AFRICA.

I love the weight of a hard-hitting rifle, and the bite of its sling strap over my shoulder, swinging in rhythm with my stride, and the sting of the noonday sun. I love the easy, murderous balance of a shotgun as it centers a fast-moving gamebird and the slam of the buttplate against my shoulder when I shoot. I love the heat of Africa, and the way the light works at a distance on the cold, blue mountains. I love the red soil and the odd, flat-topped acacias and the bulbous red trunks of the ancient, manlike baobabs. I love the yellow-barked fever trees and the oddly freighted sausage trees. I love the weaverbird nests that festoon the thorns of the nyika, swaying from their branches like shaggy, full-laden shopping bags. I love the sight of giraffes running slowly through a stand of doum palms.

I love the sand rivers and the way they sinuate through the riverine forest and the edgy feeling of anticipation you get as you round a bend and don't know what you'll see next—a band of impala or a charging lion.

I love the smell of a campfire and of the meat cooking over it and the cool green light of canvas inside a tent pitched under the trees. I love the sound of Swahili as the safari boys chatter at their work, their loud, sudden laughter, and the dying fall at the end of their sentences.

I love the African night, and the night sounds—the distant cough of a lion, the rape-victim screech of the hyraxes, baboons fretting and fearful as a leopard makes its nightly rounds, and the whoop of hyenas, the yipping of jackals....

The only thing I hate about Africa is what's happening to it.

In the foreword to *Green Hills of Africa*, Ernest Hemingway wrote, "Unlike many novels, none of the characters or incidents in this book are

imaginary.... The writer has attempted to write an absolutely true book to
see whether the shape of a country and the pattern of a month's action
can, if truly presented, compete with a work of the imagination." In short,
a nonfiction novel long before Truman Capote, with *In Cold Blood*,
affixed that label to the genre.

What I've attempted to do with these tales is to write an absolutely
true collection of non-fiction short stories, set in the same kind of country Hemingway hunted some seventy years ago, yet encompassing the
action of six separate safaris I've made over the span of a quarter century.

The stories in this collection deal primarily with hunting, but I carried
a rifle on only three of the journeys. Of the remainder, two trips were
undertaken to check out the state of the wildlife in East Africa, following
Kenya's absurd sport-hunting ban of 1976, and the rampant outbreak of
poaching that sprang from it. These were basically "photo safaris," yet
they often proved more dangerous than the hunting trips: We carried no
weapons and there were well-armed poachers in the bush. On these grim
journeys we saw large-scale destruction of wildlife and habitat wherever
we turned.

The other non-hunting safari was conducted along Kenya's tourist-
crowded "Coral Coast," from Shimoni near the Tanzanian border northward to the seedy old Arab trading port of Lamu, the last town of conse-
quence you hit before reaching the Somali line. We did plenty of big-
game fishing on that coastal trip, for black marlin, Indo-Pacific sailfish, yel-
lowfin tuna, wahoo, and giant trevally, but I've not included any of those
blue-water adventures in this book, exciting though they were. Maybe I'll
try a collection of African angling stories later.

Though this is essentially a hunting book, many of the things I saw, felt,
and learned on the non-hunting safaris necessarily shaped my moods as I
was writing. Africa is Africa, and no experience there is any less memorable than another. The country is unique: gorgeous, cruel, funny, murderous, delightful, insane, and always surprising. I've been fortunate enough
in the past forty years to hunt and fish over much of the world's surface—in North, Central, and South America, from Europe to the Antipodes,
and throughout the tropical Pacific—but Africa has always seemed to me
not of this world. It's part of another planet, I'm sure. Its huge land
mass—second in area only to the "World Island" that runs from Europe to
Asia—straddles the equator, and the sun works its full power on Africa.
Everything there takes strength from the sun. I'm certain that lions, when
they light up and fire off in a charge, are connected directly to the sun:
great boiling bundles of solar energy, just as leopards are the essence of

its plasma, filtered through jungle foliage. I've stood under giant, thirty-foot tall lobelias in a snowstorm on Mount Kenya, right on the equator, and felt the sun burning me through the clouds even as my fingers froze....

That African sun and the events I've seen transpire beneath its pitiless gaze have burned all the liberalism out of me. I've been called an unregenerate, unrepentant neo-colonialist, and maybe there's some truth to that criticism. When I first went out to Africa in the spring of 1964, as a naive young writer in the World section of *Time Magazine*, what British Prime Minister Harold MacMillan had called "The Winds of Change" were sweeping across the Dark Continent. Some winds. In their manic fury they more closely resembled tornadoes.

Britain, France, and Belgium—the major colonial powers in Africa—had been nearly bankrupted by World War II and could no longer afford to maintain their colonies. Under a smokescreen of sanctimony, they declared Africans fit to rule themselves, and beat a hasty retreat. The Africans who filled this power vacuum either cozied up to Moscow or Peking (Sekou Toure of Guinea, Kwame Nkrumah of Ghana, Julius Nyerere of Tanzania) or were assassinated in office (Sir Abubakar Tafawa Balewa of Nigeria, Sylvanus Olympio of Togo, Patrice Lumumba of the former Belgian Congo, now Zaire) or developed murderous delusions of grandeur (the self-styled "Emperor" Jean Bedel Bokassa of the Central African Republic, who literally ate schoolchildren for dinner, and later General Idi Amin of Uganda, who fed his enemies to the crocodiles), or shut their countries off from the rest of the world while establishing tyrannical regimes (Dr. Hastings Kamuzu Banda of Malawi). Or all of the above.

The white civil servants who had run Africa's colonial administrations, including their police and game departments—and run them pretty smoothly—were dismissed with what the British called "A Golden Handshake" (ie. good severance pay) as the new regimes were "Africanized." For which read "Corrupted." The first casualties of change were Africa's vast herds of Pleistocene wildlife, a legacy unique and wondrous on this overpopulated, much-battered planet.

Where the colonial regimes had enforced strict game laws, kept wildlife healthy and in balance with the landscape, and thus derived substantial foreign exchange from sport hunting safaris, the newly Africanized game departments surreptitiously declared open season on wildlife. Wardens winked at the poaching of ivory and rhino horn, taking hefty payoffs from the corrupt African officials who ran the trade—some of them leaders of the newly independent countries—in return for looking the other way. Many game wardens turned poacher themselves. They hated hunting safaris because the white hunters were always either reporting poachers to the Game Department or shooting them on sight, making trouble for everyone.

Kenya's first president, jovial Jomo Kenyatta, was believed to be a friend of the poachers. Rumor has it that his wife, the beauteous Mama Ngina (who is still alive and well and vindictive as a viper) and his daughter, Margaret, the mayor of Nairobi, controlled and perhaps still control the illegal ivory trade in that once-magical safariland. Meat poaching by the *wainanche*—the common folk—is endemic to Africa, and perhaps ineradicable, but it had at least been kept within limits by the colonial powers. With Uhuru, the wire snare and deadfall, the poisoned arrow and the AK-47 proliferated in the formerly Edenic reaches of bush and game plain.

As Washington and Moscow maneuvered for position on the African Front of the Cold War, a great spring tide of assault rifles—M-16s, Galils, H&K G-3s and AK-47s—crashed over the continent, resulting in what the elephant researcher Iain Douglas-Hamilton has dubbed "The Kalashnikov Revolution." Well-armed bands of poachers, primarily Somali *shifta* brutalized and impoverished by nearly thirty years of incessant warfare, first against Ethiopia and then against one another, roved the gamelands of East and Central Africa, killing rhinos, elephants, buffalo, giraffes, the spotted cats, and whoever or whatever crossed their paths. These were tough, pitiless, bushwise men, schooled at least rudimentarily in combat tactics, familiar with the use of plastic explosives, military maneuver, and fields of fire—as no less effective a fighting force than the U.S. Army Rangers learned to its dismay in 1993 on the streets of Mogadishu.

R OBERT RUARK, WHO WROTE THREE splendid books about postwar Kenya, *Horn of the Hunter* (1953), *Something of Value* (1955), and *Uhuru* (1962), had been declared *persona non grata* when Kenya became independent in late 1963 for telling just the truths about independence that I would witness over the next twenty-five years. Quite inadvertently I had arrived in the country only six months after Bob Ruark was 86ed from it.

In May of 1964, I stepped off a BOAC Comet jet into the humid, teeming, tin-roofed sheds of Nairobi's seedy Jomo Kenyatta Airport for a month's stay that would change my life. Nairobi—which had not yet earned the ironic nickname "No-Robbery"—was still a small, clean, pleasant city where white faces were almost as evident on the streets as black. And most of those faces, black or white, were still smiling. But already hordes of impoverished, "detribalized" Africans were pouring into the capital, living in ramshackle huts of branches and flattened milk tins in the vacant lots; break-ins and muggings were on the rise; Europeans living in the white suburbs of Karen and the Ngong Hills had to hire spear-toting *askaris* (soldiers who had had a modicum of training as tribal warriors before moving to the city) to serve as night watchmen; fierce packs of German shepherd and Rhodesian ridgeback guard-dogs patrolled the grounds of the wealthier estates after dark.

On that first trip, while cooling my heels in the offices of one sneering African politician after another, I would look out the window and, if the day were clear, see the snowcapped shoulders of Mount Kenya rising like the peaks of paradise far to the north. I visited the Nairobi Game Park as often as I could, a vast and truly wild chunk of game plain on the outskirts of town, and watched lions make a kill of an elderly buffalo, cheetahs snoozing on a rocky outcropping in the noonday sun, elephants and rhinos and wildebeest, kongoni and impala and Thomson's gazelles in the thousands.

In the evenings I hung out at the Long Bar of the New Stanley Hotel, listening to the tales of white hunters just back from safari. Each morning I woke early and went down the creaky elevator to order coffee at the Fig Tree Café on the sidewalk in front of the New Stanley. I sat at an outdoor table and sipped slowly, pretending to read the early edition of *The East African Standard* but actually watching the safari wagons load up in front of the hotel—square-shouldered Land Rovers mostly, dark green or tan, hung with big, tough Dunlop or Michelin spares of the "digger" persuasion, and the square jerrycans of water or petrol called *debes;* watched the safari boys—tall, slim, tough Samburu and Turkana and Wakamba trackers and gunbearers in crisp green shorts and bush jackets, with their lower incisors knocked out by a tribal tradition, their ears pierced and the lobes stretched so that they could drape them over the tops of their ears, or carry fat, round, wooden karanges of snuff in them—loading the clients' cased rifles into the trucks, along with veritable crates of ammunition: Remington and Winchester 7mm Magnums, .375 H&H Mags, .416 and .458 elephant loads. I listened eagerly to the Kiswahili phrases being bandied about, and memorized them. The one I liked best was *"Funga safari!"* Make ready the journey!

I knew I had to hunt....

Later in that month-long trip I finally managed to break away from Nairobi and fly up to Lake Rudolph, in Kenya's Northern Frontier District, for three days of bird shooting and fishing the hot, brackish waters of that desert-rimmed inland sea for Nile perch and tigerfish. I killed plenty of sand grouse, caught Nile perch ranging in weight up to 187 lbs. But in more ways than one it was I who was hooked. As an old saying puts it, "He who drinks from the headwaters of the Nile is bound to return."

By 1968 I had quit *Time*—burnt out on assassinations, wars, hippies, ghetto riots, and an overdose of Richard Nixon—and joined *Sports Illustrated*, to cover the safer, saner worlds of pro football, motor sports, hunting and fishing. In those days *SI*, under the editorship of a tough-minded, hard-drinking Frenchman named André Laguerre and his articles editor, Pat Ryan, was "a writer's magazine." Pat assigned stories on whatever we felt was most interesting, provided we could convince her they smacked—at least faintly—of competition. Most of us who wrote for *SI* back then—writers like George Plimpton, Bob Boyle, Dan Gerber, Tom McGuane, Jim Harrison, and Russell Chatham—didn't think of ourselves as "sportswriters," but rather as "writers who happened to write for a sports magazine." In the spring of '71, *SI* sent me back to Kenya to cover the "East African Safari Rally" a grueling, three-week long, 6,000-mile offroad race through the most rugged parts of Kenya, Tanzania, and Uganda.

The first thing I did after checking in at the New Stanley was to go across Kamathi Boulevard to a shop called Kenya Bunduki (Kenya Gun) and set up a bird-hunting trip. That weekend, before the rally began, I drove north to the Tana River and rendezvoused with a white hunter named William Henry Winter, better known as Bill, or sometimes "W.H. Troubleyou." He proved to be a short, tough, witty, and well-read Englishman, a former soldier, police inspector, and game warden who was a year older than I—as handsome (in those days at least) as a movie star, with a winsome grin, a lion's mane of thick blond hair, blue eyes that I later learned could glare like glacial ice when I'd fucked up, and a near-fatal addiction to puns and limericks. As we drove in from the highway to Bill's camp, we discussed Thoreau's nature writing, quoted back and forth from the raunchier bits in Shakespeare's ouevre, dissected the bird-hunting scenes in *Anna Karenina*, and generally decried the sorry state of the modern world.

Over the years, I've come to respect Bill Winter's judgment. Born in the English Lake District, he joined the police force at the age of seventeen and served in Malaya during the bitter guerrilla warfare of the late 1940s and early 1950s. He volunteered for army duty in Korea when that war broke out and was wounded during fierce winter fighting in the bleak mountains of what we then called "Frozen Chosen." Later he volunteered again, this time for police duty in Kenya during the Mau Mau Insurrection of the mid-1950s. Transferring to the Game Department, he served as warden operating out of Nanyuki, on the northwest slope of Mount Kenya, in the 1960s. He tracked down poachers (even then), sat up through long, cold nights to terminate the careers of stock-killing lions and leopards, and culled overabundant antelopes, buffalo, and elephants when their depredations on local *shambas* (native maize fields) became too ruinous for the tribesmen to bear. In the late 1960s, fed up with growing inefficiency and corruption in the "Africanized" Game Department, he resigned to take up professional (safari) hunting. Among his clients were Prince Bernhard of the Netherlands and Valery Giscard d'Estaing, the President of France after Georges Pompidou.

A born raconteur, naughty limericist, and incorrigible punster, Bill is also—thanks to years of experience as a game warden—a first-rate field naturalist, fluent in Kiswahili and two or three tribal languages, and a Romantic of the old school. Though his formal education ended at the age of fourteen, he has read all the classics of English literature and can quote the great poets (along with many of the lesser) from Chaucer through Shakespeare to Benny Hill at the drop of a rhyming couplet. His library of Africana is one of the best in East Africa. Blond and blue-eyed, he was the quintessential "white hunter" of African legend, a cross between Allan Quatermain and Monty Python's Flying Circus, with a touch of Evelyn Waugh in his darker mood thrown in for good measure. In 1975, the fate that stalks all African hunters caught up with him. He got out lucky, but crippled. Hunting Cape buffalo in a concession he'd leased near Narok, in southern Kenya, he'd followed up a wounded bull, only to be charged at close quarters in thick cover. He killed the buff at point-blank range but was knocked down by its momentum—one leg broken by the impact. Pinned by its dead body, he looked up and saw his client, out of control with adrenaline, aiming a *coup de grace* at the animal. "Don't shoot," Bill said. "He's finished." The client shot anyway, a .375 H.&H. magnum through the buffalo's neck. The bullet penetrated fully and slammed into Bill's leg just above the ankle. Only quick work by the Flying Doctors and many operations, both in Kenya and Switzerland, saved his life and what's left of his leg.

"Now that leg's about two inches shorter than the other," he told me later. They tell me the foot will have to come off sooner or later—not much circulation in there to speak of. But with the help of a good bootmaker I can still manage to hobble around. Not as of yore, though, Bwana, when I was young and strong and could hike all day through the African sun with nothing but a water bottle and a pistol strapped to my hip."

I've done five safaris with Bill—in 1971, '74, '78, '81, and '90. Together we've covered close to 10,000 miles of "bloody Africa," been charged by rhino and elephant and lion and buffalo, stalked by *shifta*, frizzled by ungodly equatorial heat, soaked by icy rain, stuck like pincushions by innumerable thorns, spat at by spitting cobras, and once nearly skewered by the *Silaha ya Mungu*—"The Spear of God"— which is what they call lightning in Swahili. All this was part and parcel, warp and woof, of the most powerful experience in my life. In the course of these journeys I saw East Africa change—slowly at first, and then with increasing speed, from Paradise to Pesthole.

But along the way I was also living the last of the old East African safari life, which had taken shape a hundred years earlier with the first English soldier-sportsmen who "tamed" that country. I was sharing the experiences of great hunters dead and gone, and actually meeting others out in the bush while they were still alive—Arthur Neumann, Karamojo Bell, Frederick Courtenay Selous, Teddy Roosevelt, Bror Blixen, Richard Meinertzhagen, J.H. Patterson, Philip Percival, Ernest Hemingway, and Robert Ruark, among the dead; and among the living, Harry Selby, Donald Ker, Sid Downey, Denis Zaphiro, Dougie Collins, Harry Muller, Alfredo Pelizolli, and of course Bill Winter.

"Remember, Bwana," Bill was wont to say while we were out on safari, "what you're seeing is the last of it. These tribes right now are still like your Plains Indians were a hundred years ago, wild and traditional, but it's all changing fast—it will soon be finished. *Na kwisha.* And the game along with it. Wheat schemes, tin roofs, onion farms, transistor radios, satellite television, VCRs, AIDS, assault rifles—these are the seeds of destruction that will kill this way of life, and right quick, believe me."

**T**HIS ISN'T A "HOW-TO" BOOK by any stretch of the imagination, nor is it a verbatim, journalistic account of where I went and what I shot. What I've tried to capture in these short stories is the diamond-hard csscncc of "how it was" in those last days of safari along the equator—the moods of unforgettable moments, the always-changing weather, the action and its impact on character. The only journalistic piece collected here is a long story I did for *Audubon Magazine* in 1990, at the height of the "Ivory Crisis"—the longest story Audubon ever ran, and perhaps the most controversial. The magazine's politically correct readers wrote in by the hundreds, calling me a racist, a homophobe, a male chauvinist, a neo-colonialist if not a neo-Nazi, and worse of all, a "hunter." I plead guilty only to the last, and proudly.

In the course of polishing his work, a writer necessarily leaves out certain cherished images and experiences when they don't quite fit, hoping that his craft will allow the reader to sense them even though they're absent. This is the "Iceberg Effect" that Hemingway defined and put into practice in the best of his stories. The reader sees only the tip of the iceberg; eight-tenths of it is underwater, but it's present nonetheless.

Yet as Hemingway himself wrote in the final chapter of *Death in the Afternoon*, "If I could have made this enough of a book it would have had everything in it."

If I could have made this one enough of a book it would have included:

The stormy afternoon in 1978, after the hunting ban, when—starved for fresh meat—we bought a goat from a local band of Samburu, butchered it, and feasted on it that night as the lightning flashed and the thunder exploded all around us on Naibor Keju like sixteen-inch naval gun shells; and in the morning looking out on the game plain we saw dozens of zebras and impala and buffalo lying dead—electrocuted as they stood in ankle-deep water when the lightning hit. The Spear of God had struck them. *Silaha ya Mungu*, indeed. God is a Mighty Hunter....

Or the run-in with a band of Rendile moran one festive Fourth of July as we were driving north to Lake Rudolph—bloody-minded warriors of a pastoral tribe, wild young men out on a raid—and our rifles all locked up in the traveling gun-safe, and Bill amusing them by popping the corks of champagne bottles he'd brought to surprise us on America's Birthday, which might otherwise have been this American's Deathday without Bill's aplomb....

And the *Ngoma* (dance) one evening in a Samburu village where an old man sidled up to Bill and began complaining about how silly the young people had become of late: "They aren't doing it right. They make up their own steps for the dances. And just listen to this music! It's like hyenas squalling!" Archie Bunker in blackface....

And the night at Crocodile Camp when we threw rotten chickens into the river and the crocs came up boiling through the thick, muddy water like schools of two-ton piranhas, and we lured them up onto the bank, and saw how fast we could run when they came for us, and later how the

moths swarmed around the lamplight and dove into our cups of lukewarm tea, and what it's like to swallow a soggy, inch-long, still-flapping
moth when you're not paying attention to what you're drinking....

And the time at the end of the infamous "Slip-Slidin' Away" safari when
we stopped for lunch in Narok at Nyati Hall, an old white settlers' pub
from colonial times that had now been taken over by Maasai, and the tall
herdsmen standing gloomily beside us all painted in ochre as they
swigged their beer with their spears leaning upright on the scarred
mahogany, and the barman not only had no sandwiches but had never
heard of such a thing, and the beer was warm as piss, and when I went
back to the loo to take a whiz, I found the cracked tiles of the men's
room floor carpeted with huge, human turds in every stage of ripeness....

And prowling the ghostly, red-stone ruins of Fort Jesus, the 16th century Portuguese bastion in Mombasa where thousands of Renaissance
Europeans had died under siege by the Arabs in the dawn light of colo-
nialism; and the "bugger boys of Lamu" up the coast, male prostitutes who
propositioned all and sundry with the magic words, "I have beeg pennis!"
and how Bill flashed those glacial eyes of his on them and in clipped, furious Swahili gave them what for; and Dougie Collins with tears in his eyes
recalling the old days in Somalia, up in his apartment in the Arab quarter
of Lamu, an apartment that had once been a sultan's seraglio, but now the
walls were hung with Dougie's portraits of his lovely, long-gone Somali
mistress, the legendary Amina....

And the white-haired British beldame who, while strolling the beach at
Diani where the original Blue Lagoon had been filmed, saw a naked
German tourist approaching her in full erection, and as she passed him
thwacked it with her rubber-knobbed rattan cane, and later proudly told
us, after the German had fled all adroop: "I parried and thrust, and when I
made contact there was a disgusting thump!"

And Bill's story, one evening around the campfire, of the night during
the Mau Mau Emergency when he got a frantic call from an elderly white
settler, a retired British colonel—"Inspector Winter, come quickly! The
Mau Mau have struck!" And Bill racing out through the monsoon rains
over terrible roads, armed with a Sterling burp-gun, wondering what
ghastly shambles he'd find at the Colonel's farmhouse. And the Colonel
coming out to greet him, stiff-backed and irate, and leading him stiff-
backed at double-time into the kitchen. "Just look at it, Bill—they've
stolen my pudding!"

And I should have included more of the long, wonderful walks through
the grasslands and the thornscrub and the riverine forests as we looked

for game, the jewel-like African starlings flitting through the branches and the stately crested cranes wading in hot shallow ponds, the secretary birds stalking the nyika in their endless search of snakes; vultures and eagles and marabous turning high, high overhead, the cough of lions at night, that chesty, no-nonsense sound that the Africans aptly call *"Ngruma."*

I should certainly have written more about Bill's safari-men—old Joseph who ran the camp with as little fuss and as cool a competence as the deft Wodehousian Jeeves; and the friendly presence of Wamatitu, who died recently but whose many kindnesses will never be forgotten by this Mzungu; and the wiry, happy Wachira, an ancient Kikuyu who dug our latrines and gathered firewood for our evening bonfires and was known throughout camp as "The Apprentice Firesmith," and Isaaca who always brought my morning tea, the first face in my tent: *"Jambo, Bwana,"* along with a grin and a verbal weather report— *"Iko moto, ya mvua mingi"* (It's hot and raining like hell), then took my boots away to shine them for the day's hunt; and Lambat the 'Dorobo head-tracker, always cool in a crisis and hot for blood; and Red Blanket, the sardonic, blue-black Samburu who dubbed me *"Bwana Risasi Tatu"* (Mister Three Shot) when I flubbed the kill of an eland; and slim, shy Machyana, Samburu; and the husky, unflappable, one-eyed Ayan, a Turkana, who could see with his single orb ten times more than I could with my two; and Shillingi, a.k.a. Colonel Steve Austin, whom I saw grow from a scrawny, excitable herdboy into a tall, strong, confident young man with cattle and a wife and children of his own.

And there should be a hint at least of my companions on some of these safaris—Dan Gerber in 1974 and '90, Bill Eppridge in 1978 and '81, my friend the "superhippie" David Smith who joined us in '78, Boyd Norton who shot the pictures for *Audubon*, Tony Triolo who was with me on the safari rally for *SI*, and first but not least, Priya Ramrakha who accompanied me to Lake Rudolph in 1964 and was killed shortly afterward by a sniper while covering the Biafran War for *Time*. But I opted to leave them out; including them would have made the stories too cluttered, too "journalistic," freezing these tales in time when the hunting experience in Africa is properly timeless, seamless, forever....

I took the original title of this book from something that happened to Dan Gerber late on our 1974 safari. We were running short of camp meat. I had an extra impala on my license and urged Dan, who'd hunted nothing but birds so far, to take this one—a big, barren doe if possible. He reluctantly agreed. But though he's a fine shot, he couldn't seem to hit the 'pala. Six times he fired and missed, the shots flying wide or dropping short. We re-sighted the 7mm Magnum Schultz & Larsen rifle, but everything was spot-on.

Then Lambat took Dan in on a long, careful stalk—to within a hundred yards of the doe. Dan lay prone and took a solid rest, squeezed off.... Another miss! Lambat was furious.

"I just can't do it," Dan told him. "Those big brown eyes, she's too beautiful to kill. Maybe I could shoot something ugly, like a warthog."

Lambat looked at him scornfully, and said with a sneer, "*Moyo ni moja.*" Beautiful or ugly, the heart is one. On the next shot, Dan dropped the impala. He insisted on dressing her out and butchering her all by himself.

*Moyo Ni Moja* would have made a great title, summing up what I feel about Africa—its beauty and its ugliness transcending the merely esthetic: a power as great as life itself, and life of course includes death. But the marketing people, idiots, all of them, who have no feel whatever for words, said, "We won't be able to sell the book to the Bubbas unless it has 'Africa' in the title." So I settled for *African Twilight*, a title my wife came up with—at least it suggests the trajectory of my experience on the continent. But I'll always think of the book as *Moyo Ni Moja*. If you've read this far, maybe you'll think of it that way too.

**F**INALLY THERE MUST BE ROOM here for a metaphor: The Lone Hyena of Ras Kitau. At Lamu, where we concluded our 1981 safari—the one that took us up the coral coast—I was housed in a suite that had been the master bedroom of the island's last sultan. It was a luxurious suite, with thick stucco walls, windows laced with wrought-iron filigree, gold fittings in the bath, and lining the walls were half a dozen intricately carved Arab chests that smelled of old cedar. Just outside the rear window was a narrow, winding stairway that led to a minaret.

Each morning a muezzin scaled those stone stairs and called The Faithful to prayer. I would awaken at dawn to the sound of his footfalls, wake suddenly from dreams of lions. It was barely light enough to distinguish a white thread from a black. He was a frail, stoop-shouldered man, graybearded and wizened, and he had a hard time climbing. He would stop every few steps to hack and wheeze and clear his lungs. Then after a final lugubrious hawking and spitting, he would launch into his morning summons in an harsh, clearthroated, singsong voice that still sends chills up my spine —"Allah akhbar...."

Yet even more chilling to me was the reply that answered his call, almost an echo—*oo-weep, oo-weep....oooooo-WEEP!*

I traced it finally to a desolate, scrub-grown island called Ras Kitau, located just across a narrow channel from Lamu. The plaintive song came from a lone hyena—the last of his tribe on the island.

"Oh yes, there was another a few years ago," a *dhow* captain told me, "but then she died. Now there is only the man-hyena left. He sings each evening at sundown and every morning at dawn when the muezzin calls. It is sweet, is it not? I think he is hoping to lure another hyena-woman to his bed. So far he has not succeeded."

I hope someday he will.

# PART ONE

## ONE

# ROPE OF
# GOD

*In the eroded country west of camp, a stone pillar stood beside a soda lake. It was known to the Samburu as The Rope of Ngai.*

*"Long ago," Machyana said, "there was an umbilical cord that stretched down from God's grazing lands to this very place. The skies were much lower then, and the people could see Ngai's cattle grazing among the clouds. The Samburu, Masai, and Wandorobo were all one tribe then. The country was greener and there were many lions. When the lions killed the tribe's cattle, and the children were starving, God sent blood and milk down this Rope. One day a man who had lost his cattle climbed the Rope to ask for Ngai's help. He walked through God's herds grazing among the clouds. They were beautiful cattle, big and fat, red and white, and the clouds themselves were spun of milk and blood. The whole of heaven smelled of it. He went to Ngai and asked if he could borrow a few of these cattle, promising he would replace them once they had calved and replenished his herd. Ngai said He was sorry, but He couldn't help. All of the cattle must remain in the sky, for without them there could be no clouds or sunset. All men must make their own way upon the earth.*

*"The man climbed back down the Rope. He was angry. With his sword he cut the Rope of God. Great floods of blood and milk gushed over the land, and the Rope flailed like the trunk of an angry elephant. Then the Rope shriveled and rose high into the sky, taking heaven along with it. Now the people no longer had contact with God. The man who had cut the Rope was cast out of the tribe. From that time on, he and his descendants were forbidden to keep cattle. God allowed them only to herd bees. Bees are their only cattle. These people are now the Wandorobo."*

*Lambat, the 'Dorobo tracker, nodded agreement with Machyana's story. Nearby a lone saddle-billed stork stalked slowly through the bitter soda lake—all that remained of that great flood of milk and blood.*

# The Heat of the Rain

**T**HE RAIN BUILDS SLOWLY during the day. There's nothing rash about it, except for the prickly heat it breeds, stinging suddenly in crotch and armpits when you least expect it. As the morning cool evaporates, the day stokes up and the hills on the horizon fade from blue to slate to a dirty dim brown: barely visible, glimpsed and as quickly gone. Now toward noon, as we wait for lunch, a vulture turns slowly high above the game plain, up where the air is still cool. Far below, a solitary secretary bird picks its long-legged way through the thorn scrub, stabs suddenly at the ground, and comes up with a wriggling comma—snake or lizard, perhaps a baby dragon?

The heat distorts everything. Watching the speed of the secretary bird's strike makes your eyeballs ache.

Isaaca, bringing a cold gin and tonic, shakes his head apologetically and says, *"Moto ya mvua."* The heat of the rain. The glass is already beaded with cold sweat and ice cubes—more precious than meat up here on Kenya's northern frontier—shrink visibly between swallows. Finally there's only one little gray rotting shard left and you crunch it angrily between your molars. Take that, old *Moto Ya Mvua*!

This heat has a density to it, with the weight and gravity of those fever dreams where your teeth feel like huge, gritty blocks in a flannel mouth and you can see the space between the cells of your body. This heat squashes you. There's no eluding it, even in deep shade. The Africans feel it too.

Wachira, our seventy-year old "apprentice firesmith" who spends most of each day briskly dragging in whole dead thorn trees for the evening bonfire, today decides to dig a new latrine. It will be cooler down there in the damp red earth.

N'deritu, our steady, shy Kikuyu driver and mechanic, lies under the dark blue Bedford lorry, his wrench turning in the truck's shade as slowly as the vulture overhead. Sweat drips from him like hot oil from a cracked engine block.

We had hunted out from camp early that morning, walking west in the cool dark around a jebel called Naibor Keju, then looking back to see the horizon redden with the promise of the day's heat. Light caught the jebel's blunt top and worked down the bare rock to the scrub growth where the baboons lived. Last night a leopard got one of them. We heard the leopard coughing as he came closer and closer to where the apes huddled in the darkness. The baboons heard him too and their voices came quick with fear and warning. Then we could hear them scrambling and scuttling over the rocks, looking for safer hiding places. This was hide-and-seek the way our ancestors played it three million years ago. Finally a baboon screamed—louder than a frightened child, as loud as a tree hyrax, which is the loudest animal in the African night—and the big male baboons began to hoot. Others screamed in sympathy, but it didn't help. At last, around midnight, they settled down and went to sleep. In my tent I imagined I could hear the leopard crunching bones.

Out on the plain the next morning we saw mixed herds of zebras and gazelles feeding unconcernedly in the dawn light. A band of impala bounced suddenly, like red rubber balls, along the dark edge of the thorn forest. Bill Winter stopped to glass them. "Nothing special," he said. "We can do better."

The sun boomed over the horizon, and a wave of heat rolled out from it like the blast from a suddenly opened woodstove. "Cripes," Bill said, "let's get out of this and take a little stroll through the timberlands. 'The days grow hot, O Babylon! Tis cool beneath thy willow trees.'"

I recognized the quote from O'Neill's "The Iceman Cometh." The iceman would be welcome in our camp right now. We angled down over broken ground toward the fringe of thorn where the impala had been. The grass on the slope was only ankle high, brittle and pale. Not much food value in it for the grazers, but the ground was littered with their crunchy black ball-bearings. The trackers trailed behind us, Lambat the skinny Wandorobo with Bill's .458 Remington and square-shouldered Otiego the Turkana with my .375 H&H Magnum, while Machyana, a young Samburu, carried both the 7mm. Mag and the .22 Anschutz "finishing piece."

"Could be a lion or two lying up in the thorns," Bill said. "But it's too hot and dry here for buffalo. Good thing. It's a bit close for a sudden encounter." He signalled with his hand to the trackers.

Lambat handed the .458 to Otiego and loped ahead to look for sign. He ran with an easy, loose stride, slightly stooped, his eyes slitted and mouth closed so as not to give himself away by the white flash of teeth or eyeballs. He disappeared soundlessly into the dusty green of the trees. We followed at a slower pace. The heat was gaining weight by the minute.

*"Ngiri,"* Lambat said when he came back. *"Mbili. Moja na kubwa."* He made upsweeping gestures at the sides of his mouth.

"His Lordship says there's two warthogs in there. One of 'em's got good tusks."

"It's too hot for porkchops."

"The lads like a bit of pig," Bill said. "We wouldn't eat it ourselves, of course. Too much chance of tapeworm."

We walked on. This patch of forest was laid out in long, almost rectangular clumps divided by natural alleyways that branched off from one another at right angles.

"It's like a supermarket in here," I said. "Like the aisles in the Grand Union or the Shop-Rite. All it needs is signs and specials. This way for warthog chops and knackwurst. That way for ground gerenuk and monkey brains on the half shell. What's up the next one, do you think?"

"Dik dik salami?"

But a flock of guinea fowl scurried ahead of us as we turned the corner, their feathers glinting metallic black, then candy-flake blue as they passed from shadow into sunlight, then back to black in the shadows.

*"Kanga,"* I said.

"Right. You're learning a few words now, aren't you? About time."

"Too bad we didn't bring the shotgun. They'd go nice cold for lunch tomorrow."

"Snap one with the Two-Two if we jump them again," Bill said. He took the Anschutz from Machyana and handed it to me. "There's a hollow-point round up the spout already. Just flip off the safe when you see them and Bob's your uncle."

We could hear the birds running ahead, their claws leathery in the dry grass and thorn leaves. Then I saw a head rise behind a fallen tree trunk. The rifle was up and the safety off before I knew it, and I was looking down through the peep sight without seeing it, only the front blade steady on the bird's horn-crested blue head, and *pop!* he was down, thrashing in the leaves. The rest of the birds flew, getting up heavily, with a lot of noise. Lambat ran ahead and grabbed the dead guinea by its feet, held it up, its wings still beating weakly. Blood ran down his wrist and Otiego, watching, laughed his wicked Turkana laugh.

When we got back out toward the edge of the thorn, Lambat—up ahead again—raised his hand and crouched. Then he gestured us forward, hand down and beckoning slowly.

"*Polepole*," Bill whispered. "Take it slow and easy. He sees something good."

We eased on forward in that deep Groucho crouch that always makes me want to laugh—The Marx Brothers on Safari, stalking Margaret Dumont or perhaps some big-bosomed blonde. Lambat pointed through the screening brush. A band of zebra stood feeding within two hundred yards of our cover.

"That's a nice one there." Bill said. "That stallion at the back. Do you see him?"

He was half again bigger than the mares, his stripes solid black against his bone white ground. The stripes of the mares were browner, set in pale gray. He had a good stiff mane and his ears stood up white and sharp in the strong light. I put my hand back for the .375 and felt its weight, heavy and cool in my palm.

"Better shoot sitting," Bill whispered. "Use your knees as a rest. If you try it prone you won't see over the grass."

I wrapped the sling around my forearm and mounted the rifle, sliding my forward hand back along the smooth leather of the sling until the buttplate was tight on my shoulder, trying not to think that this was a wild horse I was about to shoot. Remembering I'd promised my father a zebra skin rug, and I had three of them on my license, and they were after all Burchell's zebras, the common ones, not the increasingly rare Grevy's, and what the hell, they shoot horses, don't they? At the same time, images kept galloping up from my unconscious—whole passages from "Smoky" and "The Green Grass of Wyoming," the entire *Black Stallion* series I'd loved and read dogeared as a kid, a sudden picture of Trigger, stuffed, the way Roy and Dale had had him mounted after the great horse's death, with a gang of hippies dancing around and painting him in black and white stripes. The heat on the edge of the game plain was unbearable.

"On the shoulder," Bill said softly. "Break him down. Whenever you're ready, Bwana."

Through the 4X scope I could see him, huge and close. A wisp of white grass wriggled in his jaws, then disappeared. His eye was huge, black, and wet. I dropped the crosshairs to his shoulder.

A slow, steady squeeze....

*Whump!*

I lost him in the recoil but heard the bullet whack home. Then it was all dust and hoofbeats out there, the childhood books gone in a whirl of rumps and knobbed heads and yellow teeth, wet black eyes flashing through the dust.

It was an African Guernica.

*"Los Desastros de la Guerra:* The Movie."

And then they were gone. The stallion lay on his side in the short grass, his left front leg angled upward and quivering. As the dust cleared, the leg slid down, stiff, to the horizontal.

We went up to look at him. His eyes were glazing. His nostrils were bright pink, paling and drying now in the heat.

"Good shot."

"Christ."

"Couldn't agree with you more. But it's better clean than dirty, if you're going to do it."

"Let's get back to camp," I said. "The heat's hardboiling my brains."


**T**HAT NIGHT WE HUNG THE ZEBRA'S skinned carcass, minus a haunch and the backstraps that were drying for biltong, from a thorn tree a few hundred yards below the tents. Maybe a lion would come. Not that we'd shoot one over a bait, but it would be exciting to see a lion or two close to camp. The heat was serious even after dark. After dinner and some desultory chat, I took a cold bottle of Tusker into the tent with me to sip while I read myself to sleep. I was reading T.E. Lawrence's *Seven Pillars of Wisdom* and had come to the part about the attack on the Gaza-Beersheba line. There's a passage in there about Richard Meinertzhagen, who was on the intelligence staff with Lawrence. Meinertzhagen's is one of the great, chilling names in the pantheon of "Crazy *Mzungus"* (white men) who came out to East Africa in the early years of this century.

"Meinertzhagen," Lawrence wrote, "a student of migrating birds drifted into soldiering, whose hot immoral hatred of the enemy expressed itself as readily in trickery as violence... Meinertzhagen knew no half measures. He was logical, an idealist of the deepest, and so possessed by his convictions that he was willing to harness evil to the chariot of good. He was a strategist, a geographer, and a silent laughing masterful man who took as blithe a pleasure in deceiving his enemy (or his friend) by some

unscrupulous jest, as in spattering the brains of a cornered mob of
Germans one by one with his African knob-kerri. His instincts were abet-
ted by an immensely powerful body and a savage brain, which chose the
best way to its purpose, unhampered by doubt or habit."

I penciled this into my notebook, taking care with the punctuation,
then finished my beer and doused the Coleman lantern. Did Lawrence
approve of Meiner? Does it matter?

Toward morning it still hadn't rained, but you could feel it hanging
there in the dark. The heat was suffocating. I woke with the Three A.M.
Willies and an urgent need to take a leak. From the front of the tent,
before I unzipped the mosquito netting, I looked down to where the
zebra hung. The carcass twisted slowly, white in the moonlight, and I
could see shapes moving in the shadows near it, heavy-bodied and hump-
shouldered. The carcass suddenly jerked. There was a sound of tearing
and crunching.

Lions?

No, hyenas.

My bladder was aching.

To hell with them.

I stooped to unzip the netting, then saw something close in the shadow of the thorn tree just outside. It was blacker than the darkness, stock
still. I looked more closely and saw it was a hyena, not a big one, but it
stood there not ten feet away, staring at me. I eased on back into the
main part of the tent. My bladder ached worse than before. I looked at
the beer bottle standing empty beside the cot, but there was more in me
than the bottle would hold. It would be funny if it wasn't so damned
uncomfortable. Suddenly I was furious, angry as hell—or Meinertzhagen.
I had a *rungu* Machyana had given me, an African knob-kerri of rock-hard
heavy thornwood that tribesmen use, instead of their sacred spears, for
killing lesser game like enemy women or hyenas. I grabbed it from the
cot-side table, unzipped the tent's door and stepped out into the moonlight. I'd corner the bastards and splatter their brains... but the hyenas
were gone.

Before dawn the rain broke, crashing down in cool splashing waves,
pounding like thunder on the canvas, and its sweet smell filled the tent.
The world revived. When the sun rose, the country steamed green with
new growth.

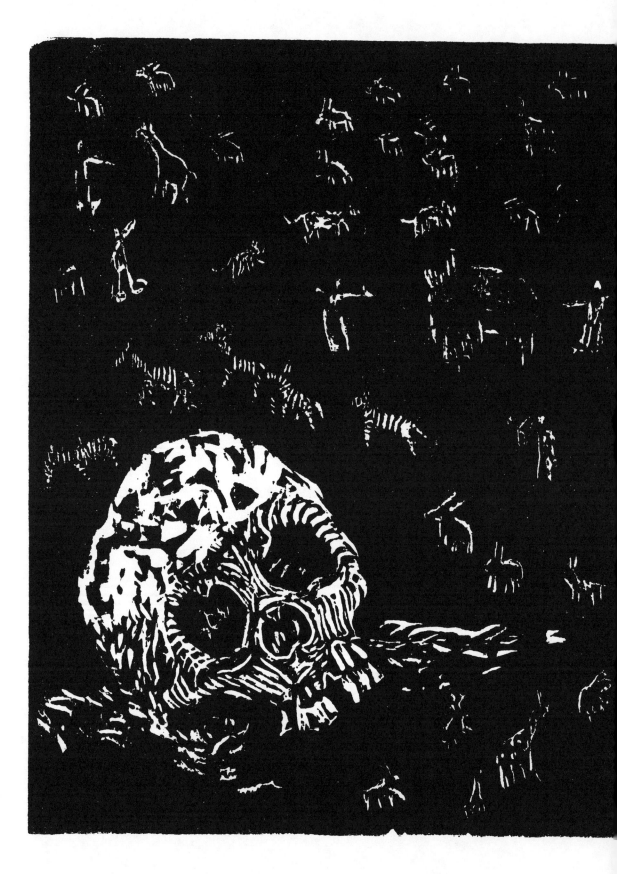

# Sepulchre

THE SKULL WAS RESTING between the roots of a thorn tree, nearly obscured by short, dry grass. Something about it caught my eye as we walked uphill, planning to scope the plains beyond for shootable game. Maybe it was the skull's roundness or its bony warmth in this cold, angular country, or perhaps just that it was human. Our eyes might seek our own kind, even (or especially) the dead.

"Look at this." Bill came over and pushed it with the toe of his safari boot.

"Small," he said. "A child, perhaps, or maybe a woman." He picked it up and stood unmocking in a Hamletlike pose. "Not smashed or shot through. But see these scorings along the sides? It's been gnawed by something. A hyena would have crushed it. Maybe a lion or leopard?"

Sudden images of kids with lollipops.

The trackers had stopped and were watching us uneasily.

"We'd best let it lie in peace where we found it," Bill said. "The boys get nervous about things like skulls and skeletons." He placed it gently back in the grass. We continued to the top and scanned the country beyond with binoculars.

There were mixed herds of zebras and topi and impala feeding in the grasslands below, and a small band of Tommies off to the side, their white tails spinning like tiny propellers. It was their spinning tails that drew the eye to them.

They're so small—a mature, well-fed Thomson's gazelle buck will weigh only sixty pounds on the hoof—and their pale tan-and-white markings with the broad black bands along the side blend so naturally into the cloud-striped dun of the game plain that without quick movement like the buzzing tail, it would be hard to spot them.

If you shoot a Tommy and his tail keeps spinning, he's not mortally hit. Only when it stops does he stop for good.

"Nothing much," Bill said, handing me the glasses. "We've plenty of meat in camp and none of those heads are worth the killing." He sat down and rested his back against a tree trunk. "But it's nice up here in the wind, hey, Bwana? A bit of a nip in the air. I'll send one of the boys down to the truck for our thermos and we'll have a nice cup of *chai*, what say?"

Lambat was cold, too. He decided to build a fire, without using any of those sissified Mzungu matches. He searched the hillside for a slab of soft wood, not punky but soft enough to frazzle under steady abrasion. Then he cut a stick from one of the thorn trees and rounded the end to a dull point with his knife. He piled dry grass on the wood slab and began spinning the upright stick back and forth between his palms.

Where it bit into the slab, curls of sawdust ridged outward. A few tendrils of smoke began to show, then more and more as the friction heated the fine sawdust.

When it began to glow dull red, Lambat delicately eased his dry grass closer and blew on the coal—gently, gently, shading the coal from the wind with his body.

Then there was fire.

In five minutes he had a crackling blaze going. Then he balanced a thin plate of shale on the stones surrounding the flames and set our tea to warming. With a blazing stick from the first fire, he built another over in the lee of a rock. He and the other trackers gathered around it to warm themselves while we drank our strong, black *chai*.

"Whose skull do you think that is?"

"Hard to say. Could be a herd boy, like one of those kids we met up on the Tinga Plateau, jumped by a lion one day long ago whilst tending his flock. Or a girl or a woman out gathering firewood. Or an elderly person abandoned during a migration—a 'Dorobo perhaps, some of them are quite small. They usually build a ring of stones around the abandoned one, and cast spells to keep off the hyenas, but I don't see any stones here. I suppose we'll never know. This whole country is paved with bones, human as well as animal. Paved in bones and cobbled in shit. Petrified antelope dung for the most part. And it's so dry up here in the north that the bones keep bloody near forever. Look what Leakey and Johanson have been finding up near Lake Rudolph. Skeletons of protohumans three and a half million years dead. Yes, Bwana, the whole of Africa is an open-air sepulchre."

"Let's take it along," I said. "It deserves a better burial place than this."

"Well, you'd best not let the lads see you take it. They don't care for ghosts prowling around camp."

I lingered behind as Bill and the trackers started back down the hill
and slipped the skull into the game pocket of my hunting coat. Back at
camp I hid it behind a duffel bag in my tent and forgot about it. We were
busy hunting and exploring the country.

One evening we went out after tea for a walk around the kopje, looking to knock over a decent impala from the bands that fed on the far side.
"The *dume* of a 'pala band is a busy fellow," Bill lectured as we strolled
along. "He gathers his females in season and keeps them to himself, in
constant battle with the same forces that beset us humanfolk. His wives
are forever wandering off, looking for a brighter bit of green someplace
out there where the lions wait. Innocent enough but a bit unwary. Not
quite street-wise enough. You know the old Milne poem about James
James Morrison Morrison Weatherby George Dupree's poor mother? 'She
tried to get down to the end of the town. Forty shillings reward.' The old
'pala ram must chase his errant ladies and shoo them back with the rest
of the harem. Meanwhile, the young bucks who've been lurking around
the edges, waiting for the old man to get distracted, dart in to grab a poke
while he's not looking. Back he comes at a gallop, hooking like mad with
those lyrate, needle-sharp black horns, and sometimes the young stud
stands up to him. Then the hills rattle to the clash of horns. All this, a
hundred times a day during the rut—it hones the old *mzee* down fine.
He's all head and horn and balls and frazzled pecker before it's over, his
body wasting down to something sad, a loose hide covering bitter meat.
Just like us old codgers, hey, Bwana?"

In the course of those evening walks we saw some epic battles. This
night, following uphill toward the clatter of horns, we found a dominant
*dume* slugging it out with a challenger not ten yards from us, where we
lay unseen in the brush that fringed a clearing. The females scarcely
looked up from their feeding to see how their lord and master fared. Two
of them calmly chewed grass while being serviced by a pair of the challenger's bachelor-band buddies who'd snuck up on the *mzee's* blind side.
The older buck was clearly losing the fight.

"He's not bad, the big one," Bill whispered. "Good balance and spread
to those horns. Just about over the hill now, I'd say. Not half bad." He
turned and looked at me. "Why don't you take him?"

"Poor old fucker," I said. "He's losing it, isn't he?"

"Yes," Bill said. "Let's play God. Take him."

I slipped the 7mm Schultz & Larsen forward and braced it sideways on
a thin thorn trunk. The old 'pala had backed away from the younger one

now, and through the scope I could see him looking toward the females. They were not looking back at him.

He dropped to the shot.

"There's something a bit nasty about that," I said later, while we were gutting the old buck.

"How do you mean?"

"Well, killing them during the rut while they're preoccupied by sex."

Bill laughed ironically.

"Would it be more honorable to kill them while they're eating? Or sleeping? Or going to the loo? Come on, Bwana. It's killing and none of it's pretty. Next time you come out here we'll try to run one down on foot and you can bite it to death. But I'll bring along plenty of Spam, just in case."

On the way back to camp we found the Meat Cave. Bill spotted an overgrown trail leading up through the bush to the steep north face of the kopje. It seemed unlikely that hoofed mammals had made it—their turf was more open country, where their eyes and legs protect them. We followed it up. The track ended at the cliff wall where a narrow slot opened out within the rock to a dark passageway.

It led downward in smoothly worn natural steps toward a musty, darker black. I felt like Allan Quatermain about to meet She Who Must Be Obeyed, or Tarzan entering the Lost City of Opar. Gold and a nubile temptress? Or cobwebs and frightened bats....

My Zippo lighted the way down into a low chamber with barely enough headroom for a painful crouch. Charred stones formed a fire ring round a heap of cold ash.

Crude figures painted in fading ocher decorated the walls. They depicted spindly men with spears and drawn bows killing spindly antelope and rough elephants and lions that bristled with arrows, blood spilling black from their mouths or from wounds that looked like mouths.

"It's a Meat Cave," Bill said, his voice hollow in the hollower darkness. "The hunters came here in the old days to eat meat and make magic to kill more *nyama*. Doesn't look like it's been used in a good long while. Maybe the *mzees* who used to come here are all dead now, or moved to the city, and the young men don't believe in the old magic anymore. Now all they have is the magic of corrugated tin roofs and the Sony Walkman and the Toyota *motokaa*."

THE CAMP WAS IN AN UPROAR when we returned. One of the staff, in sweeping out my tent, had found the hidden skull. Within minutes of the discovery, the assistant cook had cut his hand peeling potatoes, a coal jumped out of the fire Wachira was just starting and landed on his bare foot, and one of the skinners, walking out of camp on urinary business, nearly had his eye poked out by a long thorn on a branch that struck at him—viciously, like a *nyoka*, a snake—even though there was no wind. This was *mbaya sana*, very bad to the very worst degree.

"We'll have to get rid of that skull," Bill said. "Or we'll have a bloody mutiny on our hands."

"Let's take it up to the Meat Cave."

"Good thinking."

Dark was falling fast as we hurried up through the thorns with our ghastly burden.

Bill had the open-sighted .458 slung on one shoulder and I carried a twelve-bore shotgun loaded with SSG buckshot—insurance against hyenas or leopards. When we found the cave mouth again, only the faintest ribbon of dirty red light hung on the western horizon. Bats and nightjars hawked for moths in the cooling air. We paused for a breather at the cave mouth.

"I wish we'd brought a flashlight," I said.

"Sorry."

We eased down into the cave. The Zippo guttered weakly, went out, came back afire with reluctance. Warmer air inside the cave was rising up the steps into the cool of the falling night, a moldy breeze that smelled of bat crap. There was a rustling sound ahead of us and I pointed the twin muzzles of the shotgun straight ahead—I was leading—with the butt clasped tight against my hip with my elbow, thumb on the safety, trigger finger on the guard. "Don't bloody shoot no matter what," Bill whispered fiercely. "That SSG will bounce around in here like shrapnel. And the blast alone will blow out our eardrums." Then he giggled, dryly.

Two bats came flapping past us. One's wings brushed my face.

We put the skull in the ring of stones, dead center, then raced back up and out, into a night pierced by jackal howls and the friendly roar of a lion. Back at camp, all was peaceful once again. No one had suffered so much as a bug bite since the skull left the premises. The assistant cook's cut was not only mending but he was sitting up and taking nourishment. Wachira's foot didn't hurt anymore, and even the skinner was smiling. We could hear him chanting a work song as he fleshed the impala's hide. Dinner was oxtail soup, medium-rare buffalo fillets, boiled red potatoes, and for dessert, the inevitable Three Six Five—canned fruit salad, so named because you eat it every day of the year on safari—but ambrosia-cally transformed this evening by a hefty dollop of Devonshire clotted cream.

Later we sat beside Wachira's fire and sipped strong Kenya coffee, black and rich as the African night. The world was sweet again.

Except....

"Maybe I can sneak that skull back out of the cave before we leave."

"Don't even think about it, Bwana," Bill said. "These lads take such matters seriously and it's not for us to make light of them. Anyway, if you want to fetch it, you'd have to go it alone. I've had enough of these night sweats. And I'll tell you just what would happen. You'd go sneaking up there in the dusk, just as we did before, but when you neared the cave you'd see firelight flickering dimly through the entrance. Weak flames, feeble and pale as a white man's soul. You walk up closer, as if mesmer-ized, and peer into the cave. You see dim shapes hunched over the heat-less flames, muttering and mumbling their meat prayers. If you're polite—and I know you are, Bwana—you'll call out a quavering 'Hodi?' May I approach? And a weak, hollow voice will answer something inscrutable, like 'Karibu!' Enter. If you have the knackers for it—and I know you do, Bwana, you'll duck through the entrance and make your slow way down that incline, down through the swooping bats, coming closer and closer to the fire. Then one of the figures will turn, shadowy and draped in stiff, mildewed skins. The smell of rotten meat will fill the cave. A mummified arm will appear and gesture to you, like this."

He made a slow, creaky, beckoning motion.

"And then the dry, dead voice again, 'Kariboo—Kaaa-reee-booo!'"

"'Come near, my friend, come near.'"

The skull remains in Africa.

# The Shame of Risasi Tatu

WE WERE HUNTING THE GIANT FOREST NYALA, a rare man-eating antelope the size of a moose and with horns to match. I'd never felt worse in my life. So far everything had gone wrong that could go wrong, and things were growing worse by the minute. I'd wounded the animal hours ago and it made off fast, belly low to the ground, snarling like a gut-shot lion. The bolt wobbled loose in the receiver of my rifle, the safety wiggled back and forth as freely as a molar after a fistfight. The rifle barrel was sprouting blossoms of rust, though I'd oiled it only minutes earlier. The steel itself felt soft as warm taffy. The light in this thicket was dim, the color of an old sepia-tone print, and wherever I tried to focus, my vision blurred. The trackers were clearly frightened, but I couldn't follow their whispered warnings or see which way they were pointing.

We broke out of the forest into the edge of town, with a blood trail evident now as we crossed a pot-holed highway through fast, heavy traffic, dodging fleets of huge and heedless eighteen-wheelers while suburban matrons screeched mutely from their glossy station wagons and cops ran toward us with angry billyclubs. The blood took us past a railroad station where a commuter train was just pulling out—a train I'd have to catch or else lose my job—but we followed on into a big lumberyard, edging our way tensely around giant stacks of two-by-fours. Bodies lay everywhere, torn through with holes the size of .50 caliber bullets, limp and flat as only dead men lie. A strong, hot wind set the stacks of lumber to swaying. "Remember," Bill kept saying, "they bite, they bite." But I couldn't see or hear anymore. The Giant Forest Nyala was there, its horns as big as a Christmas tree, but I couldn't see it.... Not for the life of me....

I'd picked up a touch of fever the previous day, along with a case of what the Brits so eloquently call "The Squitters," and when I awoke from the dream I felt limp as those spectral dead men. It was late afternoon by now, time to hunt again. I splashed lukewarm water over my face and walked to the mess tent for tea. The sky had clouded over, low thick clouds the color of steel wool, and the air was wet and heavy. You had to suck it in. Wamatitu poured me a cup of hot, black *chai* and I gagged down a couple of Lomotil pills to placate my angry bowels.

"The lads were out scouting while we had our lie-down," Bill said. "Spotted a nice band of eland just down near the edge of the forest. A good bull among them. What say?"

Eland, I thought. Nice big target. Even though I still felt as shaky as I had in the dream, I could hardly miss an eland, could I? A whole, placid ton of gray-clad, sweet meat, tender as Kansas City beef, enough to feed even our voracious, thirteen-man camp crew for a solid week. We'd seen plenty of eland already in that country, grazing peacefully, unwarily on the plains in herds mixed with zebras and Grant's gazelles. With their huge wobbly dewlaps and shoulder-humps, they look no more difficult to stalk or kill than a herd of Santa Gertrudis cattle. Almost unsporting, I thought, to hammer so gentle a creature. But I had one on my license and we certainly did need the meat.

"Let's do it."

We bumped on down from camp toward the southeast, past the Samburu village where children ran out as usual to chase the safari truck, laughing and screaming with delight as Bill threw them handfuls of hard candy—as usual. The truck rode rough on the smoothest of highways, and I felt my lunch cavorting like the Flying Wallendas as we bounced over pigholes and rain-eroded termite mounds. Bill called the truck the "GT," or "Green Turd" more formally. It was a revamped Toyota Land Cruiser, much tougher and more readily repaired than the old Land Rovers that once dominated the East African safari game. The only problems we'd had with it during that entire month-long safari in Kenya's truck-eating Northern Frontier District were flat tires—or *"punk-chahs,"* as the Africans called them. But the lads were so accustomed to thorn-inflicted punctures that they could change tires like an Indy pit crew, with time left over to check your water and oil.

Beyond the village we hit a rutted two-track that angled off toward the edge of the forest. Bands of Tommies grazed in the short, sun-shriveled grass, looking up unconcernedly as we passed while their tails spun like helicopter rotors. None of them bolted. They seemed to sense that we were after something meatier than Tommy chops. The sky dropped lower and lower as we neared the forest, and the highlands to the east disappeared in a tendrilous mist. A figure loomed ahead, tall and black and spiky with spear points. It proved to be the biggest, ugliest, scruffiest tribesman I had ever seen. A traveler, judging by the tattered, grease-stained red blanket that he wore wrapped across his bony broad shoulders, *shuka*-fashion, and the beat-up British Army musette bag he carried. His skin was much darker than that of the coffee-colored Samburu of this country, and his bone structure heavier. Most backcountry Africans look taller than they actually measure because they are so slim, but this man stood well over six feet from his calloused, thorn-scarred size fifteen triple E feet to his massive, heavy-jawed head. He carried two spears, a *simi* and a *rungu*. Ready for trouble, sure enough. We stopped to talk with him.

"Claims to be Samburu," Bill translated, "or at least he's been living among them long enough to speak the lingo. Says he can speak Suk, Turkana, and Rendile as well. He'd like to join up with us. Could come in handy when we head north through that Rendile country. I don't know a word of their tongue, nor do any of our lads."

So the man we called Red Blanket joined our merry band. That's Africa for you, at least away from the cities—no resumes required, no checking on references from former employers, no lengthy, meaningless job interview by some flunky in Personnel. Just size the man up and if he looks good, hire him. That must have been the way it was a century ago in America, in shops or lumber-camps, on ranches or whaling ships or backwoods pig farms. Red Blanket was a journeyman in a dying tradition.

He began to earn his keep right away. He had seen the eland we were seeking, just a few miles back, and could take us to them directly. Which he did. They had not moved far from where our scouts spotted them earlier. We stopped half a mile away and glassed them through the thin acacia scrub that masked us. Creamy gray blobs moving slowly, massive among the quicker movements of the zebras they'd mixed with. The zebras whisked their tails nervously, barking now and then at one another, bucking or trotting off in startled indignation when biting flies got under their cruppers. Two young stallions reared and thrashed at one another in mock combat. Gangly foals nursed hungrily as their mothers grazed. The mixed herd was feeding from our right to our left, and I glassed the eland carefully for the big bull.

"There," Bill said at last. "Toward the front. He just came up from that lugga—maybe there's water down there, or perhaps he was digging for roots."

The bull was half again bigger than any of the other eland, so large that his heavy, twisted black horns looked short against the rest of his bulk. These were the common or Livingstone's eland—called *Pofu* or *Mbunju* in Kiswahili—smaller and more abundant relatives of the increasingly rare giant eland that once ranged from Senegal to the Bahr el Ghazal in the war-ravaged Sudan. Browsers rather than grazers, they tame fairly easily. Semi-domesticated herds of them have been established in South Africa, Zimbabwe, Texas, and even in southern Russia. Just as well they're gentle, I thought. I'm too damned fragile today for something that runs both ways....

We moved toward the herd in a fast semi-crouch, using the low thorn-brush for cover, stopping when one or another of the animals raised its head to stare in our direction. Otiego stayed close on my left, carrying the .375. A light drizzle began to fall. The droplets felt hot as fire on my bare arms and legs—fever, I thought. My head was light with it and my neck was beginning to ache. I could feel my bowels begin to clench and during a pause I shook a few Lomotils into my palm from the bottle in my shirt pocket and choked them down dry. Bill watched me.

"You feeling okay, Bwana?"

"Good enough for this," I said. It sounded cocky, contemptuous, and I suddenly felt more rotten than ever. The weight of the steel-wool sky felt like the worst of luck.

"That tree," Bill whispered, pointing ahead to our left. "Good cover. Close enough."

We crawled the last hundred yards, picking up the inevitable thorns in our knees, then lay flat behind the fallen trunk. The herd hadn't seen us yet. What wind there was came from them to us and I could smell the sweet, sickly barnyard reek of them in the wet air. The big bull was maybe a hundred yards out, feeding toward us at a shallow angle. An easy shot. I slid the rifle cautiously over the tree trunk and found a solid rest—both elbows planted, sling wrapped, forend gripped solidly in my hand, resting firmly on the thorn bark. I looked at him through the 4X scope. He filled it—a slatey grayish tan with that short brown-black mane down the back of his neck and the faint white stripes cutting vertically from his spine toward his belly.

"There's a round up the spout," Bill whispered. "Take your time and whack him out."

I looked up from the scope, wiped my forehead with the back of my hand.

"Where should I hold on him?"

"The way he's broadside to us now, just back of the crease," Bill said. "Heart and lung will do it."

I dropped my head back down to the scope. The crosshairs lay sharp and black on the gray and white striped ground. I edged them across so that the vertical hair just touched the crease behind the animal's left front leg.

Safety off.

Squeeze.

Steady.

*Whump!*

"Kee-rist!" Bill yelled as I bucked to the recoil. "You've killed a bloody zebra!"

I looked up fast, horrified. Sure enough, through the dust of the wheeling, galloping herd, the groundshaking tom-tom beat of their hoofs, I saw something small and gray lying flat on the plain. A zebra mare, limp as the dead men in my fever dream.

"I don't...How in the hell?" I could hardly talk. My head ached from the recoil and the awfulness of it.

"Maybe you shot clean through him," Bill said, getting up now. "She could have been standing just beyond him."

But his voice sounded doubtful.

We looked at the fleeing eland. The big bull was at the head of the herd. He ran straight at the hedgelike barrier of a thornbush thicket and then leaped it—six feet, straight up, easily as a steeplechaser in the Grand National.

That animal had not been shot. As we walked over to the dead mare, we passed a warthog hole. I felt a sick, sad urge to crawl right down into it and curl up, forever.

"No blood," Bill said, scuffing his boot where the eland bull had stood when I fired. "You bloody well missed him. You bloody well killed a sodding *zebra*. And a lady one at that." His voice was hard, tight, controlling his anger. His eyes when he looked at me were glacial ice. From nearby came a high, plaintive squeal. As the dust cleared I saw a zebra foal standing perhaps a hundred yards away, stamping its tiny black hoofs, shaking its wobbly head, whinnying pitifully, then screaming again.

"That's her young 'un," Bill said. "Poor bloody little orphan." Bill pressed the mare's swollen teats with the toe of his boot. Pale blue-white milk leaked out and dribbled down into the dust-thickened blood beneath her. I looked for the entry wound. There it was, just where I'd held, behind the shoulder.

Then it came to me.

After I'd zeroed the eland through the scope, I'd looked up to ask Bill about shot placement. The muzzle of the rifle must have swung off target, not much, but enough. Back down on the scope, I'd seen gray lined with dirty white stripes—the same colors on the zebra mare as on a bull eland. I hadn't checked the whole animal, not at that range—not much more than seventy-five yards.

I had made the worst mistake a hunter can make.

I had not been sure of my target.

And on an open game plain to boot. The zebra foal screamed and whinnied again.

"All right," Bill said. "Let's go after him."

He gave quick orders in Swahili to the trackers and we headed out along the trail of the eland. "Even though there's no blood, and even though he ran like he hadn't been hit, there's still a slim chance you hit him," Bill explained. "We have to check it out."

The orphaned foal skittered away as we passed it, then trotted after us for a while. It stopped, whinnied, then turned back toward its dead dam.

"What'll happen to it?" I asked.

"No worry, Bwana," Bill said curtly. "A lion will nail him tonight, no doubt. Or maybe a hyena."

The eland had disappeared to the west around a range of low, brush-grown hills a mile ahead. The trackers trotted quickly on their trail. Lambat, the keenest tracker, ran on ahead on a shortcut over the hills, hoping to spot them from the high ground. He disappeared over the brow. Ten minutes later he reappeared and signaled us with his arms.

"They've hooked around to our left, over the hills," Bill said. "They're milling around in a group, calming down. We've still got a good chance."

Our pace slowed as we entered the brushy country beyond the first hills. Lambat had rejoined us and led the way. A hundred yards, two hundred, then he crouched with his palm down and signaled us forward.

*Polepole. Very slowly.*

As we came up on them a cow spotted us and grunted. They spun and ran.

The big bull was at the rear this time, big as a house. I swung on him as he ran in that stiff-legged slashing trot of theirs, holding him hard in the center of the sight picture, then swinging forward through his lolloping shoulder. I didn't even feel the shot this time. He rocked to it, staggering, knees buckling, then caught himself and ran on into thicker cover.

We ran after him. There was blood where I'd hit him, a big arrow-shaped splash of it bright red on the hoof-slashed dirt. We pushed flat out into the thorns, feeling them hook and rip at cloth and skin but with no sensation of pain. I felt hard inside now, headache gone, vision sharpened with the adrenaline of the chase, blood pumping hot and *kali* now, fierce with the need for his death, for some minim of atonement. I was ahead of them all, running stride for stride with Lambat.

He pointed ahead into the next copse. The eland bull erupted from it, lurching as he ran with the wound I'd given him, and I fired again, seeing the dust puff from high on his side, just behind the near shoulder, under his hump. He crashed forward in a nose-dive, ploughing up the dirt as he skidded. His hindquarters swung around with the momentum of his fall and he lay on his belly, front legs folded under him.

I stopped short of him, waiting for Bill to come up.

"All right," he said.

The bull's head was swaying from side to side, his big brown eyes glazed but unseeing or staring inward, perhaps, to the onrushing void. His head looked a yard wide. The horns still seemed small, though they would measure close to twenty-five inches. Bill took the .22 Magnum Anschutz from Otiego.

"Finish him," he said, handing me the rifle.

It took three shots in the sticking place, just at the base of the skull, before his head finally dropped.

B Y NOW THE RAIN WAS FALLING HARD. Hard and cold. Darkness was coming on fast when the truck pulled up. I was shivering uncontrollably in the wet dusk.

"You'd better get in the truck, Bwana," Bill said. His anger was gone, but not my shame.

"I'd rather see it." The boys were gutting the eland now, the stench of hot blood sweet in the chilly air, great steaming coils of intestines as thick as firehose piled on the ground, and a gray-green paunch that looked the size of a Volkswagen. The boys had the eland over on his side and his empty body cavity gaped like a cave entrance in the afternoon gloom.

Red Blanket, all six feet and more of him, was squatted inside the eland's rib cage. I could see the flash of his knife as he pared fat from the ribs, then the shine of his teeth as he gobbled it raw. He caught me looking at him and stared back, unsmiling, his knife and his feeding hand doing their work automatically. The pooled blood in the eland's chest reached nearly to Red Blanket's ankles.

He shook his head slowly from side to side in the metronomic rhythm of the bull as he lay dying.

*"Bwana Risasi Tatu,"* Red Blanket said. "Bwana Three Bullets."

There was no humor in it. Just the truth.

Driving out later I asked Bill to stop the truck on a slope near the spot where the tragedy began. I got out and glassed the game plain. The nine-power lenses sucked in what remained of the light and I saw the carcass of the dead zebra mare lying flatter than ever where I'd shot her. Then I saw the colt waiting patiently just beyond her.

Farther still, on the very limits of the light, darker than the night itself, three clumsy, slope-backed animals paced back and forth, waiting even more patiently for dusk, and the final act.

# PART

# TWO

# NECKLACE

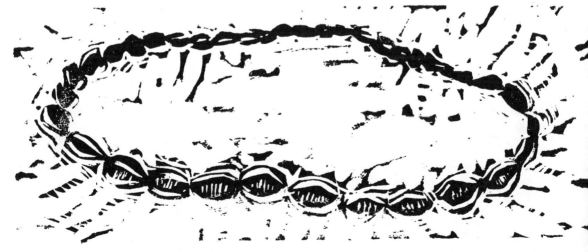

"I know that elephant," Lambat said.

The elephant was standing across the valley at the edge of the forest, watching us and fanning his shoulders with his ears. He was a small bull, but an old one by the size of his ivory. The tip of one tusk was broken off about a foot back from the point, and his head was huge for the size of his body. He had rolled in the mud and then the rain had come so that the red of the mud was striped across his back. His legs were a solid, unbroken red.

"Zamani—*many years ago, in the old time*—that elephant killed my friend," Lambat said. "It was in the time when we were moran, *soldiers.* When you are moran, *you may not eat or sleep alone. You must sleep and eat with your brothers, the men of your age class, and you may not sleep with a woman. Later, when you become* mzee, *you may marry and sleep with a woman, and eat with her, or alone if you like. But if a* moran *eats alone he may come to believe that he can travel alone, and then he might die. That would not be good for the people.*

"My friend was in love with a girl. He knew he could please her if he bought some beads he had seen in a village on the other side of this mountain. But there were elephants on the trails that crossed the mountain, even as today. It would take my friend a day and a night and another day to make the safari. He asked us, his brothers, to come with him on the safari. Otherwise he could not go and get the beads. At first none of us would go with him. Then some of us agreed to go."

We were sitting in the shade watching the elephant and hearing the story.

"We crossed the mountain and saw that the elephants were there. But they did not kill us. Still we were frightened. In the manyatta across the mountain, my friend bought the beads; they were a necklace, they were very fine. As we were coming back it got dark. The rest of us decided to spend the night sleeping in the trees off the trail. We were afraid of the elephants. But my friend went on. We warned him not to go. But he wanted to show the beads to his sweetheart. On the trail he met this elephant. This very one that we are seeing now.

"This elephant—this very elephant—tossed my friend and tusked him and knelt on him and broke his ribs and legs. Then this elephant went away. In the morning we found my friend. He was still alive. He asked us to look for the beads he wished to give to his girlfriend, but we could not find them. When we came back to tell him, we could see that he was na kwisha. *But he was* bado kufa, *not yet dead. He asked us to go to his girlfriend and see if the elephant had carried the beads* to her. Then he died. We crossed the mountain to our manyatta and asked his sweetheart if she had the beads. The elephant had not brought the beads to his girlfriend. We never found the beads."

I looked back at the elephant. He was still staring at us, tossing dust from the ground over his back, his eyes red, ears flaring and flapping backward, then flaring forward again.

"How do you know this is the same elephant?" I asked Lambat.

"Oh, you can tell," Lambat said disdainfully. "This one is an elephant who has stolen someone's beads."

All this was told in the toneless voice of truth.

"Well, he's too small for us," Bill said. "Only about fifty pounds a tusk, and one of them's broken. God will have to punish that elephant, for thievery if nothing else. As He should all of us."

# The Virgin's Eyelashes

**W**E STOPPED AT A HUT beside the two-track for news of the country. It was dawn on the equator, but at an elevation of eight thousand feet. The three Africans who lived in the hut stood shivering beside the Land Cruiser, taking what warmth they could from the ticking engine block. Their faces looked gray in the overcast light. Water dripped from the thatched eaves of the hut. Two of the men were laughing at the third. He was old, and under the togalike wrapping of his faded red *shuka* we could see a dirty bandage on his shoulder. There were long black-crusted scabs on his face and forehead. He was very angry. He kept gesturing toward the forest, shaking his head in disbelief at the effrontery of whatever had mauled him.

Bill Winter listened attentively, arms folded across the chest of his trim corduroy safari shirt, one hand stroking his freshly shaven chin. He was wearing what I thought of as his Scotland Yard Face. He'd been a police inspector in Kenya before joining the Game Department. Then came "Uhuru" with its many changes, and Bill had been "Africanized" into the free enterprise system as a Professional Hunter. He finally turned, still suppressing a smile, and translated.

"This *mzee* says he was grabbed by a lion last night. The others think it very funny. The old man doesn't. They say he was drunk and fell asleep outside the *nyumba*—the hut—and the *simba* came and picked him up by the shoulder, there where the bandage is, and carried him off into the forest, but even then he didn't wake up. This *mzee* says he wasn't drunk, that he screamed when the lion took him but these rascals were too frightened to come out and help him fight the lion. He says he punched the lion in the nose until finally it dropped him. The *simba* slapped him on the face in rebuke—you see the claw marks—and ran away. Even then these men did not come. He had to crawl back by himself."

"What do 'these rascals' say?"

"They say the *simba* was actually a *fisi*—a hyena—and it dropped the old man when they came after it with torches."

"What do you think?"

"Hyena," Bill said. "If a lion had actually clawed him, the old man wouldn't have a face anymore. It would have peeled off like one of those rubber masks in the movies. But something mauled him, sure enough."

"Then what the hell were you smiling at while the old man was talking?"

"I don't know, Bwana," he said, grinning fully now. "I just love it how angry some people can get over things they can't control, and how much joy others will take in their woes. But we'll patch the old fellow up and make it all better." Bill looked under the bandage and showed me the puncture marks. The holes were puckered and purple in the dusty dark brown skin, two of them on each side of the shoulder, leaking pale pink fluid. Lambat fetched the first-aid kit from the back of the truck and Bill worked sulfa powder into the holes. The old man didn't flinch.

Then Bill bandaged the wound with sterile gauze and tape, and gave the man a handful of tetracyline spansules. He told the *mzee* how often to take them, emphasizing that he mustn't take them all at once or they would lose their magic. The old man nodded, all smiles now, his few brown teeth as ugly as his wounds.

"*Nyama iko?*" asked the men. Is there game?

"*Ndio.*" Yes.

"*Wapi?*" Where?

"*Huku.*" They gestured widely all around. There was indeed game, everywhere hereabouts. There always was, to hear the locals tell it.

"*Mbogo iko?*" Are there buffalo?

Indeed there were. Up on the plateau, where the people graze their stock, and in the dongas where the plateau falls off into the forest. Yes. *Mbogo mingi sana*. Very many. A few of them gigantic—*kubwa sana*.

WE DROVE UP THROUGH THE DRIPPING FOREST, tires spinning and smoking sometimes on the steeper grades where the black-cotton soil was slick as grease, steam rising from the hood and leaking out the trail like dragon-fire. Then around a high wood-grown knob where the ragged gray bottoms of the clouds seemed to touch the trees, and then back down again to where the track forded a stream. The water was fast and brown, full of leaves and twigs and dirty brown foam.

Across the stream the track rose again toward the gloom of the sky, and one of the trackers pounded the flat of his hand on the cab roof, a signal to stop. They had seen something.

Machyana, whose country this was, jumped down and ran ahead. He bent over some dark lumps that lay steaming in the middle of the track and stuck his forefinger in one, then ran back proudly with the finger held high before him. Rather like an Olympic torchbearer. He was the youngest of the three trackers, a handsome lean Samburu of about twenty, and this was the country he had grown up in. His face was excited. *"Mafi ya mbogo,"* he said.

"Buffalo shit," Bill translated. "And very recent at that. It's still hot. Care for a snort?"

"I'll take your word for it."

We got out to look at the tracks. They were like cow tracks only twice the size, and they led across the road and up into the dense forest from right to left. The piles of dung steamed sweetly in the cold. It smelled like a cow barn in winter when you go in at milking time, and the smell of the buffalo themselves still lingered in the air, but stronger than the cattle smell, wilder. Or perhaps it was just anticipation. Lambat studied the tracks and told Bill something.

"He says this bunch are moving, they won't stop till they get up into the grass where they can feed. It wouldn't do us much good to follow them up on foot from here. Better to forge on to the top and look for them up there. He says none of the bulls are especially *kubwa.*"

At the top the forest thinned and opened out into a broad rolling plain of knee-high grass. Far off to the right, near the edge of the forest, we could see the low dark line of a *boma,* the fence of thorn scrub that encircles an African backcountry village to keep predators out at night. The rounded roofs of the *nyumbas* rose above the thorn tangle and curls of blue woodsmoke from cooking fires flattened downwind. There were humpbacked cattle grazing in clusters across the plain, each small herd guarded by boys armed only with sticks. They watched us big-eyed as we approached, holding their sticks in their hands like the older ones, the *moran* or warrior class, held their spears, impassive. Again a hand slammed on the rooftop. Machyana shouted something to Bill.

"Those two boys just ahead are his kid brother and his cousin," Bill said. "We'll stop for a filial reunion."

Machyana leaped down before the truck had halted and ran ahead. The two boys suddenly broke into bright smiles, their eyes lighting up with surprise. The taller boy, who turned out to be the cousin, was named Leteyan. He was husky and cocksure. The smaller was Machyana's brother Piringin. He was thin and wore a flimsy *shuka* that looked like a discarded red-and-white-checked cotton tablecloth.

"Machyana's father died awhile back," Bill said, "probably of TB. His mother's not been able to remarry. Too old. She's all of thirty I suppose. It's a hard life for a widow among these pastoral tribes with no man to look out for her. There's not much sharing among these people. Look at Piringin there, the little bugger's about starved to death. But at least his big brother sends home a few shillings now and then."

The boys said there were buffalo over at the far side of the plateau, a big herd feeding at the edge of the forest. They would take us to them. Machyana said no, they must stay with the *ngombes*—the cattle—that was their duty. He knew the place they meant. He would find the *mbogos* himself. The boys' faces fell. Bill said not to worry, we would be back. He took a bag of rock-hard candy from the glovebox of the truck and gave them each a handful. "I'm the Candy Man," he hummed to himself as he climbed back behind the wheel: a jolly blond clone of Sammy Davis, Jr..

The boys watched us out of sight, their mournful mouths full of sweets.

By the time we stopped again the clouds were beginning to burn off. A few patches of hot blue opened and closed in the fast-moving sky. Where the sunlight hit the earth the effect was surreal—a split screen version of Paradise, in both Technicolor and black-and-white. Red Blanket, the big, craggy-faced Samburu who had adopted us on the afternoon of the botched eland, handed down the rifles to the trackers and stayed with the truck. We walked toward the tree-line through wet grass that soaked our camel-hide safari boots. Machyana ran on ahead to scout for the buffalo. Knobs of gray and pink rock stuck out of the grass, and a big eagle flapped off from the top of one and climbed up into the wind.

"Verreaux's eagle," Bill said. "See the white rump patch?"

We climbed the rock to see what he'd left, and found the picked bones of a small warthog. The short, tufted tail hung by a thread of gristle from the severed spinal column. We watched the eagle until it was only a speck against the sky, then looked out over the country. You could see the forest dropping away steeply to the east and north, fading into solid black and then sharply ending at the tan haze of the game plain. Far off to the southeast, a line of blue hills rose in a series of humps like elephants' backs to disappear into a huge mass of cloud that Bill said masked Mount Kenya.

Machyana came back with news. The buffalo were just over the lip of the plateau, feeding in the open woods on a north slope that fell off steeply into heavy timber. He had seen only cows and calves, a few young bulls, but many of the 'bogos were hidden by the trees. He could climb one and throw some sticks in there and maybe move them.

Okay.

We took positions in the trees above the open slope where the cows and calves were grazing. I could see them moving black and slow, just their backs and an occasional upsweep of shiny horn tips showing above the pale green filter of the grass. Bill was about twenty yards to my right, holding the binoculars ready at his chest, the wind ruffling his thick mane. To my left stood Otiego, stock still against a tree trunk, watching. He had my rifle. We could see about two hundred yards downslope to where the tops of the trees marked the dropoff. I felt something bump against my boot. It was a dung beetle pushing a ball of shit, trying to roll it up over my foot. It was as big as a golf ball and perfectly round. It would be fun to collect a pile of them, I thought inanely, take them home, paint them white, and scatter them in the rough at some swank course. But I lifted my foot and let him roll on.

A heavy stick whirled out from the top of a tree to our right and fell silently into the foliage below. No response. Then another. I could see Machyana's arm swing and the top of his tree sway. The second stick fell short just like the first. Then Machyana threw his *rungu*—his thornwood knob-kerri. It spun up and out, heavier than the deadwood he'd thrown earlier, and crashed far below. The hillside erupted with charging black bodies. Cows and calves below us spun and fled, followed by an avalanche of bigger buffaloes. The ground shook with their weight as they ran.

"Quick," Bill yelled, "let's get out where we can see 'em."

We ran down the hillside through the grass after the herd, dust rising thick where they'd kicked it up, no sound but the pounding of hearts and hoofbeats, and as I ran a shaggy brown shape came galloping past me, high-rumped and hunched, its short, straight, twisted black horns laid flat along its neck. A bushbuck. The buffaloes poured down over the edge of the dropoff and disappeared into the trees.

We stopped and listened to them crashing below.

"There was a good *dume* with them," Bill said. "A good bull. Forty inches anyway."

"Did you see that bushbuck?"

"Indeed. Good thing he didn't take a poke at you. They're bloody aggressive little beasts." He walked over to me, grinning merrily in the dust. "You'd have had holes in you like that old man this morning, but of a larger caliber."

"Should we go after the buffalo?"

"I reckon not," Bill said. "They're alerted now, probably still moving, and it's too bloody thick down there, they'd hear us coming a mile away. We'd practically have to kick them up the jacksy to see them, and there's always the chance that some grouchy old cow would ambush us. All told, Bwana, this is a situation where discretion takes precedence over valor."

"What if they'd stampeded up our way instead of downhill?"

"Then young Machyana here would be scraping us off the floor with a spoon right now." He translated the exchange for the boys and they laughed. Machyana, who had retrieved his *rungu,* led the way back uphill.

We stopped an hour later for lunch, having seen no more buffalo on a slow, circling hike along the edge of the plateau. Lambat built two fires, one for us, one for them, and while our fire heated water for tea, theirs was charring spare ribs. They were the ribs of the eland I'd shot the other day, and while we ate crusty sandwiches of the *Mpishi's* camp-baked whole wheat, lettuce, and cold, thinly sliced Tommy tenderloin, the trackers ripped at their ribs. Each rib was nearly three feet long.

"You ought to get a picture of that," I told Bill. "It'd make a great come-on for your Texas clients, what with their love of barbeque."

"Looks mighty tasty all right, podner. Why don't you ask old Red Blanket to share one with you?"

Red Blanket was hunkered back on his heels in the lee of a rock, his brows furrowed as he stripped long pieces of fire-blackened meat from the bone, his teeth flashing as he chewed. A trickle of blood ran down his chin. He looked up balefully when he saw us watching him but didn't smile.

"I think I'll give it a pass."

After lunch we lay in the shade of the trees, reading or dozing while the trackers went out on foot to look for buffalo sign. They returned an hour later with Piringin, Leteyan, and an old man from the village. The old man wore a pair of enormous British Army combat boots that had seen better days. One sole flapped loose from the toe and the other boot was missing a heel.

"The boys say they've located couple of good bulls to the south of here," Bill said. "Old 'Bogo Boots here says he knows where a fine one's lying up not far away. At the edge of a *donga* just over there." He pointed to the northeast.

"This *dume* has an *askari* or two with him—that's a couple of smaller, younger bulls that act as guards, keep the old outcast company, and warn him of danger. He's lying up in a thicket at the far edge of the draw. 'Bogo Boots says he saw him not an hour ago."

'Bogo Boots nodded, unsmiling.

"Which one should we go for?"

"I think we ought to go with the old man," Bill said. "The boys may have seen something all right, but to them any bull would be a huge one. This old timer knows buffalo. He wants some *nyama*—some meat—and he knows we'll give him some if he puts us on a good buff. He knows he'll get damn-all for a wild goose chase. I'll sent Otiego and Machyana with the boys just to see if they've got anything. We'll take Lambat and go with this *mzee*. Maybe we'll get lucky."

'Bogo Boots led us at a quick pace over the rolling downs, past strangely shaped rock outcroppings that leaned crazily, like an African Stonehenge, against one another in the strong, rich light of the waning afternoon. The grass was sharp-edged, rasping against our bare legs. A flock of francolin scurried ahead of us through the grass but didn't flush. A few wind-bent trees—thorn and candelabra—stood scattered at the edges of dry watercourses. Basking lizards flicked their tongues from the rocks and then simply disappeared before you could look again.

We stopped just below the crest of a grassy ridge. Lambat and 'Bogo Boots crept up to the top and looked over. Lambat came back in a tight crouch.

"He's down there, all right," Bill said, whispering now. "Lambat says there's a *donga* between us and him. He's in heavy bush just the other side of it, about two hundred yards from the top of the ridge. He sees a way we can get down and just across from him without him seeing us. The wind's in our favor."

I looked uphill. The grass on the skyline was bending in our direction, blowing from the buffalo to us.

"Lambat says he's a good one. Let's go."

I cracked the bolt of the .375 H&H Magnum to make sure there was a round in the chamber. There was. Three and three-quarter inches of brazen death, tipped by a 300 grain solid. I knew the numbers on the bullet. It would leave the muzzle at 2,550 feet per second—a little more than 1,700 miles an hour—and generate exactly 4,333 foot-pounds of energy. A little over two tons. A good-sized bull would weigh just under a ton; in places his hide can be two inches thick. Beneath it, a collision mat of tough powerful muscles capable of tossing a four hundred pound lion twenty feet through the air, or punching a blunt black horn tip through the sheet-metal side of a safari wagon like a fingertip through pie dough. Between the horn tips lies a corrugated skull cap of heavy horn that can turn a bullet or crush a man's chest like an eggshell if the buffalo gets him down. Bill had told me that buff like to kneel on a man when they drop him, then lick his face like a giant housecat for the salt in his blood, sweat, and tears.

That tongue is rough enough to rasp the skin away in a matter of minutes. Licked to death by an angry *mbogo*....

But outrage is *Syncerus caffer's* middle name. Phlegmatic, wary, deceptively ox-like when undisturbed, he deeply resents any disruption of his daily routine. Let me eat my fill of grass, he says, wallow in the mud, mount my cows in season, and hammer the young bulls who challenge me for breeding rights. Mess with me, though, and you've had it. No other member of Africa's Big Five—elephant, rhino, lion, leopard, and buff—has so formidable a reputation for vengeance.

Wounded, he will slope off into the heaviest cover he can find, then circle out to right or left of his track and lie in wait for whatever hurt him and is brave—or foolish—enough to follow him up. His mastery of the flanking attack has been equaled in modern times only by Stonewall Jackson and Norman Schwartzkopf. When he comes, it is fast and hard from close range, head held high (thereby denying his hunter a shot into the shoulder hump that could break the buff's back), his nostrils flared like cannon muzzles, the long hairless barrel of his body—a powder barrel, a tun brimful of the meanest, fieriest popskull ever distilled—caked with mud and dung, his eyes locked dead on revenge.

The only way to stop him then is to put a bullet up his nose.

It is best to avoid the necessity of such a shot.

To do this, you must get in close, as close as you can, to ensure a steady, accurate first shot. One that will catch the buff totally by surprise and shatter his bones, lungs, and heart before the adrenaline starts pumping. One of the great Zen lessons of hunting dangerous game is that you must put yourself into the deepest peril simply to avoid a worse peril. You must get so close to *Bwana Mbogo* that you can see the ticks crawling on his earholes. That's where we were headed.

Lambat angled through the grass up the blind side of the ridge, moving fast and quiet in the Groucho Slouch. I followed, with Bill bringing up the rear. A big rock reared near the crest of the ridge and we used it as cover. Water seeped from beneath the rock and drained down into the *donga*, its steady moisture supporting a man high growth of reeds and scrub for a hundred yards or so, until the water played out and grass again took over. We eased down through the green stuff, trying not to let our boots suck in the mud. At the end of the cover we had to crawl, infantry style, through the grass for another twenty-five yards before a rise of ground masked us from the buffalo's eyes. I still hadn't seen him, but he was in the heavy scrub not fifty yards from us now. The wind was steady and strong from him to us, muffling any inadvertent noise we made. Then there were bushes again and Lambat got up into the crouch. We cut back to our right and down, following a faint game trail that led into the *donga*. Lambat stopped. He looked intently across the shallow brush-choked daw. Eyes slitted, lips tight, his skin positively glowing coffee-brown with the intensity of the stalk.

Bill moved past me to Lambat's side. They stared into the green gloom. I followed their eyes.

He was there.

AT FIRST I SAW ONLY THE OXPECKERS, hopping and hissing in the thicket, a flash of sunlight illuminating the thick red bills and the yellow rings around their eyes. Now and then they clattered their beaks. If I could see the eye-rings of the buffalo's tickbirds, we were close. Then I saw a tickbird hanging upside down, feeding. And then the *mbogo* himself popped clear. The bird was hanging from his chin, nipping blood-swollen ticks from the buff's lower jaw. The big quiet bulk of the animal filled the far side of the draw, dark hide mottled with light and shadow into near-perfect camouflage, not twenty yards away. His head was up, jaw moving as he chewed his cud. The eyes were dreamy, big as baseballs, forelegs folded under him like a cat.

Bill slid back over to me.

"See him?"

"Yes."

"Hard to sock him right, lying down that way. The birds will see us sooner or later, then he'll get up. If you hold on the bulge of his shoulder, you'll not go far wrong—break both it and his spine. That's the way we want him. Down and out."

I nodded.

"Can you do it, Bwana?"

I nodded.

"I'll be backing you with the .458, just in case."

I nodded.

Bill moved away. The buffalo stood up.

I was sitting with my elbows on my knees. Sling wrapped, muzzle forward, finger on the trigger guard, safety off, the buffalo filling the 4X scope, crosshairs steady on the round shiny slate-gray bulge of his shoulder point, finger on trigger, deep inhalation, slow outflow. *Bam-whap*— the explosion of the bullet so loud it almost drowned the heavy wet clubbing sound of the hit.

Then the buff was running straight toward us.

"Sugar!" I heard Bill's rifle bang and saw his bullet tear shrubbery just over the buffalo's hump. Clatter of working bolts. The trees across from us shook.

Oxpeckers flared and flapped. He was angling to our left a bit.

Then we heard a heavy crash and a long drawn-out mournful bellow. And a long, sad silence.

"Music to my ears," Bill said. "His death song."

"*Na kufa,*" Lambat said. "*Kabissa. Piga mzuri,* Bwana." He held out his limp, skinny hand for a shake.

"*Asante,*" I said. He was dead all right, completely. But I wasn't sure how good the shot had really been. He'd run on us. Not far, but he'd run.

"Did you hit him?" I asked Bill.

"Don't think so. He'd have gone down right then if had. I think I saw leaves fly just over his shoulder when I shot. No, it was your bullet that did him. We'll see when we dig it out. But crikey, for a moment there my bunghole was twittering like a virgin's eyelashes."

When we went over to him we found him lying just at the edge of the *donga*, head-down, his right horn tip hooked into the roots of a sapling. Below, the gorge deepened, sinking down abruptly into a tangle of heavy vine and brush. That's where he was headed when he died. If he'd gotten in there, we'd have had to go in after him. There is no such thing as leaving a wounded animal untracked, unfinished, in African hunting. You hurt him, you kill him. It's not just a sporting tradition, but a practical consideration as well. A wounded animal is doubly dangerous. Anyone who might come near him as he lies wounded and hurting, his grudge against the world building to murderous proportions, is going to taste his wrath. It's the professional hunter's duty to undertake this distasteful task, and the client can stay behind and let him do the dirty work. In fact, many hunters prefer it that way. Without the clumsy client tagging along, they have less to worry about at the crucial moment. Some clients I'd heard of had developed strange, sudden stomach aches or trick knees when the time came to follow up a wounded, dangerous animal. I'd like to think I wouldn't, and that Bill would let me come along.

But I was glad, in that moment, with the buffalo lying there quiet and scabby with his ticks crawling around his earholes and his heavy black horns catching the lowering light and the tickbirds clacking a dirge for their master, that I hadn't had to test the proposition.

Lambat loped off to get the truck and the others. The *mzee* had come down from the ridge and stood talking to Bill, his hand resting familiarly on the buffalos rump, one long wrinkled finger absently flicking turds out of the *mbogo's* poop-chute. The moment of let-down was at hand. I felt it wash over me, dark and heavy as the dead buffalo himself. It is probably nothing more mysterious than the inevitable crash that follows an adrenaline high, and I certainly didn't feel anything like regret at having taken the buffalo's life. By the same token, I didn't feel particularly proud, either. In the lingering echo of the bull's death bellow, I felt drained of both energy and emotion.

When the truck came, we tied a nylon rope to a nearby tree trunk and secured it to the buff's hind foot. Then the lads went to work caping out the head, removing the hoofs to be mounted as bookends, the tail for a flywhisk and, tomorrow, oxtail soup, the backstraps for filets. The *mzee* promised he would make me an authentic Samburu buffalo-hide war shield from the skin. Bill and I went up to the truck. He poured me a jigger of Johnny Walker—"Scottish Wine, you know, the old S.W." He handed me the flattened bullet, recovered from the bull's far shoulder blade. It was a .375, all right.

As I sat sipping the whiskey, Piringin and Leteyan came up the hill carrying the bull's sawed-off feet. They were dipping the marrow from the severed bones with long dry straws, then licking it off like ice-cream. The cup shook, splashing Scotch down my hand.

Lambat came up the hill next with the head of the buffalo balanced across his bony shoulders. The cape hung down his back, his arms were bronzed with dried blood, and with the buffalo's great black horns swooping up and out above his own head, the buffalo's dead blackness merging with Lambat's live blackness, he appeared in the eerie evening light like some cruel and powerful bull-god born of the racial unconscious.

Later, driving down from the plateau in the blood-red sunset, heading for the warm comfort of the plains, we saw a herd of elephants, perhaps sixty of them, crashing their way up a hill to our right.

Effortless, strong, heading upward toward the last of the light. From the rear of the truck came the smell of stale blood.

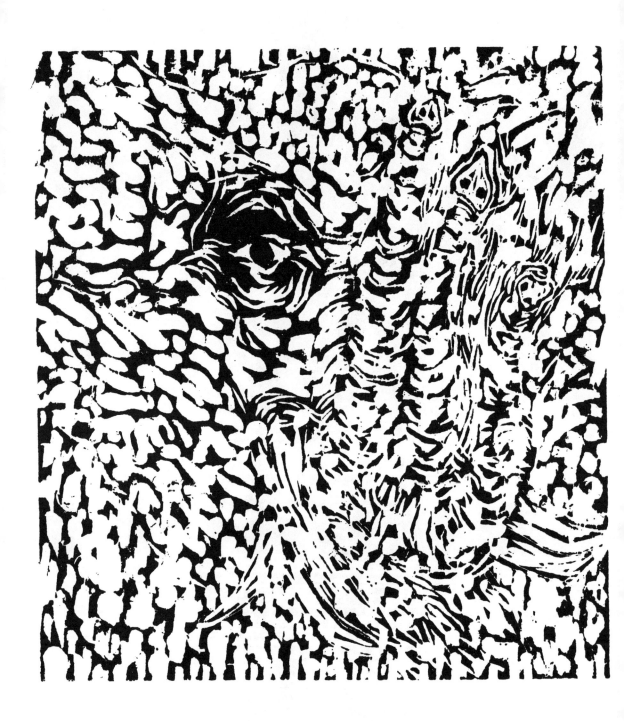

# Old Ivory

OVER THE YEARS I'VE THOUGHT again and again about the Treasure of Nyama Yangu. It's become for me, finally, the *reductio ad absurdam*—half metaphor, half punchline—of what I was seeking when I first set foot in Africa nearly thirty years ago. The rare desperate thing that will make a man rich, one way or another, or kill him in the process; the essence of wild country, the elusive meaning of safari. Or perhaps the pratfall of a lifetime....

It began quietly enough. We were having our afternoon tea in the shade of the mess tent when we saw the old man coming up the hill. He emerged from the edge of the forest and made his way slowly up the rutted red cattle track. Samburu girls in their brass and cowries and smoky leather aprons moved out of his way as he climbed, then resumed their flirting conversations with our safari boys. The old man had only one leg. He wore a faded khaki field jacket over his wraparound *shuka,* and a shapeless black fedora was pulled down low over his eyes, but he grinned with all his teeth. Under one arm was a rude crutch and in the hand of the other a glossy black walking stick that caught the low afternoon light and winked with every thump of his crutch.

"Look at that poor old *mzee,*" Bill said. "He's hiked all the way up here on one leg just to have a chat with us. It must be nearly a mile from the *manyatta.*"

Down below us on the edge of the forest, the breadloaf huts of a Samburu village rose from the thorn scrub. Women were up on the domed roofs applying fresh cow dung to weatherproof the huts against the impending rains. They slapped it on by hand, like wet plaster. At this distance you couldn't smell the dung or the woodsmoke, or hear the incessant buzz of flies, and the *manyatta* looked quaint, almost idyllic, in the sundown light.

"*Hodi!*" the old man yelled as he approached.

"*Karibu!*" Bill yodeled back. "Draw near!" Then quietly: "Poor old blighter, he'll probably ask us for some *dawa*—some medicine—to make his leg grow back. But he'll settle for a handful of APCs."

Bill was wrong, though. The old man's name was Lesombolo, he told us, and once he had eased himself down into a camp chair, his effluvium rolling out around him as warm and powerful as his smile, he asked nothing of us. Leaning forward on his walking stick, he offered us a challenge, a journey into unknown country fraught with hazard and the promise of possible wealth or, failing that, at least of knowledge. All he wanted was to come along and show us the way.

My Swahili was just good enough to follow the initial exchanges—as predictable in any meeting with tribal Africans as the Introibo and Kyrie of the Mass—but I noticed that as the conversation accelerated (leaving me far behind) Bill was paying full attention. The name "Nyama Yangu" cropped up again and again.

"Well now," Bill said at last. "I suppose it's remotely possible." He waved to Wamatitu, the assistant major domo of the mess tent, and asked him to bring the old man some *chai* and *tumbaco*—tea and the strong, stringy black chewing tobacco beloved of all backcountry Africans regardless of age or gender. "Our friend here says that when he was just a lad he worked as a safari boy for Nyama Yangu. That was what the people called old Arthur Neumann when he hunted this country for ivory back around the turn of the century. He says that before Neumann left on his last trip to the Coast—must have been around 1906 or so—he buried something in a cave up in the Lorogi forest. A couple of old foot lockers, very heavy. Nyama Yangu was most secretive about the cache. He took only four of his lads up there with him—two of them to lug each chest, so Nyama Yangu had to carry his own *bunduki*—a .577 Gibbs double rifle it was—and they all sweated a lot on the journey. Lesombolo here was one of the porters. The country is fierce, he says. Full of hungry leopards as big as lions, giant forest hogs the size of his *nyumba*—his hut—and elephants taller than the trees. When they'd buried the chests, Nyama Yangu swore them to secrecy, an oath replete with the slashing of forearms and the mingling of blood. Were they ever to return to that cave, he warned, they would die most awfully. His spirit would see to it."

Lesombolo smiled now—he must have known some English—and patted the stump of his leg, dark and shiny as old ivory where it protruded beneath his *shuka*.

"*Ndio*, yes." Bill nodded gravely to the old man. "I'm coming to that. Some years later, when Neumann didn't return from the coast, Lesombolo and the others let their curiosity overcome their caution and returned to the cave. Nyama Yangu must be dead by now, they reckoned, and anyway his *dawa* probably wouldn't work after all, he was a *mzungu*—a white man. But no sooner had they reached the mouth of the cave where the chests were buried than a monstrous elephant appeared out of the very ground as it seemed. It snatched two of the men with its trunk, quick as a flash, and brained them against the cliff, tusked the third through the chest with a *pembe* as thick as a tree trunk, and then came for Lesombolo. He ran as fast as ever he could, but the elephant was gaining on him at every stride. In desperation he leapt for the lower branch of a tree and pulled himself up into it. The elephant's trunk, though, caught him by the ankle. It paused before snatching him out of the tree, and stared at him with fiery red eyes—the eyes of Nyama Yangu. But Lesombolo drew his *simi* —his short sword—from the scabbard at his hip and with a tremendous, supernaturally powerful blow, severed his own leg at the knee, then clambered, bleeding, to safety. He stanched the flow of blood with a crude tourniquet and hid, shivering in great pain and delirium, for two days and two nights before the red-eyed elephant went away. Then he cut a rude crutch for himself—this very one we see—and made his way back to the *manyatta*."

We sat silent for a moment, Lesombolo's ancient, glittering eyes darting from one to the other of us, waiting.

"So?" I said.

"So he wonders if we'd care to go up there and dig for the chests. He thinks he could find the cave still, it's next to a big bald rock face on the west slope of the escarpment, and there's a tree with Nyama Yangu's initials carved in the bark nearby. But with his bum leg we'd have to drive him in the *motokaa*."

"What do you think?"

"I suppose it could be ivory. The old timers used to wrap it in green hide and bury it in a safe place until they could hire enough porters to carry the tusks down to Mombasa. When Neumann came out for the last time, or so I've read, he didn't have much ivory with him. The new game regulations had just been promulgated—first ever in this country—and he may have been over the limit. He was a queer old duck by all accounts.

Very possessive. Nyama Yangu means "My Meat,"which is what he told
the Samburu when they came by expecting to share in his kills. He also
apparently suffered from agoraphobia—fear of crowds. An old pal of his,
the artist J.G. Millais,said that Neumann could face a wounded lion or a
charging elephant without raising a neck hair,but he was afraid to cross
the road in Piccadilly for fear of the traffic. Toward the end,he reckoned
everyone was out to get him,even the people who wanted most to help
him. Clearly paranoid. What drove him out of East Africa was the game
laws. He couldn't bear regulation. But the long arm of *m'zungu* law—
the Great White Judge Who Takes the Fun Out of Everything—had finally
reached him. He wrote to Millais about his sorrow,just before he left that
last time. Went something like this: 'The prospect of leaving my country
and giving up the life I love makes me sad. I know so well the misery of
feeling like a fish out of water,with neither part nor lot of anything at
home. Here in my 'nowhere'I have been happy. If I am compelled to
lead a life of stagnation I shall soon get old.'"

Bill paused and sipped from his teacup,then made a face. It had
grown cold.

"What happened?"

"Maybe he buried some of the tusks from that last hunt—as this old
man suggests. Then went home to buttoned-up old Blighty and died."

"How did he die?"

"Suddenly," Bill said. "Mysteriously."

"Suicide?"

"Could be. Or just plain heartbreak —a man out of his time and
place."

"Let's go up there," I said. "Let's go up to the cave."

Old Lesombolo smiled.

"*Ndio, Bwana,*" he said.

I had a hard time falling asleep that night. My blood was up. First
there was the prospect—a long shot,at best—of retrieving a sizeable haul
of old ivory cached in the cave by Nyama Yangu more than half a century
ago. In those days the average tusk taken from this corner of East Africa
was much larger than today. We might realize a considerable sum of
money for the old ivory,more than enough to pay for another safari. The
price of ivory had nearly quintupled since Neumann's day,cspccially for
large tusks. There was no way of knowing,of course,that by 1989 it
would soar to nearly $200 a pound,thus raising the price for an average
tusk of seventy-five pounds to $15,000.

But more important than this mere monetary windfall was the chance that the side trip to the cave might put me in intimate, deadly contact with elephants once again. I'd killed one already on this safari, a herd bull with tusks of 68 and 76 lbs., stalking up close to him in thick, dry thorn-bush that made every step potentially my last, should I happen to snap a brittle twig; the tracker and I surrounded by a drowsing herd of ele-phants, their stomachs rumbling in ruminative, sleepy conversation; slip-ping closer and closer to our bull until he loomed up before us in this hot, airless thicket like the side of a craggy, ocher-stained, mossy cliff, then making out finally his long-lashed, half-closed eye—he stood broadside to us—and his earhole; laying the bead of the iron-sighted .458 on the slight depression midway between eye and ear, inhale, steady, squeeze on the slow exhalation.... *Wham!* The bull dropped to his knees at the shot, stone dead—more than six tons of him—and literally bounced when he hit. The rest of the herd was gone in a roll of thunder. As Captain Chauncey Hugh Stigand wrote back in 1913: "There is something so fasci-nating and absorbing about elephant hunting that those who have done much of it can seldom take any interest again in any other form of sport. Everything else seems little and insignificant by comparison."

No wonder I couldn't sleep.

**W**E LEFT BEFORE DAWN the next morning, pounding along the rutted track through the shadow of the forest, unseen creatures large and small crashing away through the undergrowth at our guttural approach. "'The wood is full of shining eyes,'" Bill intoned as he wrestled with the steering wheel, "'The wood is full of creeping feet, The wood is full of tiny cries; You must not go to the wood at night.'"

"Whose is that?"

"Henry Treece," Bill said between bounces. "'The Magic Wood.' Fine poet. Good advice."

Lesombolo, bouncing in the back seat with the trackers, grinned and said, *"Ndio, Bwana."*

But the night soon gave way to African daylight. Butterflies danced, red, green, blue, gold, on steaming piles of elephant dung. Colobus mon-keys stared down on us from the canopy as we climbed slowly higher and higher, through many switchbacks, toward the escarpment. Buffalo fled through a clearing. A rhino and her calf contested the way briefly, chuffing and pawing the mud until Bill stopped— "Oh shit, if she gets that horn under the frame, over we go...."—and eased away in reverse. Quick

roiling streams cut the trail in places and one of the trackers waded ahead
with a staff to probe the depth. Not to worry. Bill gunned the
*motokaa*—our jolly green Toyota Land Cruiser with its armor-plate "safari
box" sides—through the roaring brook, rifles clattering in their racks,
engine yowling, steam rising with an incongruous civilized stink from the
hood and exhaust, until we were safe on the far side. "All done as if by
mirrors," Bill said. "The G.T. knows the way."

Toward noon we stopped for sandwiches—cold, thin-sliced buffalo
tongue and sharp English mustard on slabs of fresh bread baked the previous evening in camp by our excellent *Mpishi* (cook)—washed down with
hot, sweet black tea. The tiny campfire kicked out sparks and bitter black
smoke. It was cold in the shade. Shivering on the equator. I hiked down
the track and spotted the pad marks of a big cat. Lion? Here in the deep
forest?

"Leopard," Bill said, coming up beside me. He stroked his chin as he
stared down at the tracks. "Bloody big one, too. I've rarely seen a larger."
He looked up at me and smiled. "What did the old man say? 'Leopards as
big as lions'? He wasn't stretching our legs too far, Bwana."

After lunch we forged on, losing the track at times, finding it again
with the aid of the lads, skirting blowdowns, at one point having to break
out the axes to chop our way through a wind-felled hardwood thick as a
fat man's waist. Around one bend we came on a group of huge, lumpy,
pig-like animals covered with long, coarse black hair *"Hylochoerus mein-
ertzhageni,"* Bill whispered, stopping the G.T. "The Giant Forest Hog in all
his glory. A sounder of them, no less. Not quite as large as the old man's
*nyumba,* unless he lives in substandard housing, but good-sized by any
reckoning. The old paterfamilias—see him there? The big feller with the
thick callouses under his beady little eyes. Must go nigh on six hundred
pounds, I'd guess. This species didn't become 'known to science,' as they
say, until 1907, when Captain Richard Meinertzhagen of the King's African
Rifles manage to plug a few in the Aberdares and sent them off to the
British Museum. This is wild country, all right. Otherwise the *watu*—the
tribesmen—would have finished them off by now. The hogs raid their
*shambas,* and Africans are all always hungry for a nice bit of pork, however ugly the package."

Now the trail widened, trod deep by eons of elephant traffic. We made
good time. The old man's smile had vanished as we came closer and closer to the escarpment, which loomed over us like a gray, furrowed brow—
fissured and crenelated to the face of an elephant, if you looked at it
through animist eyes. I noticed that Lesombolo's right hand was locked

almost white-knuckled around the walnut forend of Bill's Winchester .458, the only *dawa* that would work against Lesombolo's nightmare.

As the forest thinned with elevation we began to see game. Thick-necked waterbuck the color and almost the size of Montana elk, but with ringed, forward-arching horns. Little bands of impala glowing red against the greenery. Reedbuck like North American whitetails except for their recurved horns. Now and then a stocky, shaggy-maned bushbuck, almost black at this altitude except for the white blotches and stripes radiating downward from its back, and always poised near the edge of some seemingly impassable thicket into which it could disappear with near magical speed.

Bill stopped the G.T. when we spotted a nice one.

"You've got a bushbuck on your license, Bwana, and yonder stands a fine specimen. What say?"

We slipped out of the truck on the lee side, rifles in hand, and began a quarter-mile stalk. Bill had the .458—you never know, especially in country like this—and I carried my Remington 700 BDL in 7mm. Magnum, with its left-handed bolt to accommodate my southpaw nature. Lambat led the way, flitting in a silent, sinuous half-crouch from bush to bush, taking every advantage of dead ground that the terrain offered. The wind, what little there was of it, was in our faces. Lambat stopped, knelt, peered over a slight rise, then gestured for me to come up beside him. *"Huko,"* he whispered. "There he is." I peeked through the grass.

And there he was. We'd chambered rounds in the rifles when we got out of the truck so there was no danger of the bushbuck spooking at the sound of the working bolts. He stood head up and staring in our direction, not two hundred yards away. A wisp of grass sprouted from the corner of his mouth, twitching as he chewed. The horns looked good—thick, twisted, heavily keeled. I held on the vee at the base of his throat for a raking shot, the sling firmly wrapped on my forearm, the butt and comb tight on shoulder and cheek, safety off, squeeze—*Bam!* At the impact the bushbuck backflipped; when we stood, all we could see were his legs stretching and quivering upwards from out of the grass.

*"Mzuri,"* Lambat said. *"Na kufa."*

Good shot. He's dead.

"Never knew what hit him," Bill said.

We walked over to where the bushbuck lay, his eyes already glazing. A beautiful animal. Thick-coated, muscular, heavy spiral horns. He'd weigh about a hundred-twenty pounds and the horns wouldn't measure more than two feet in length but he was, as Bill said, "a good specimen."

"It's almost too easy," I said.

"Only with a tracker like His Lordship here," Bill said, slapping Lambat on the shoulder. "And we can certainly use the meat. We may have to spend the night up here."

I looked upward. The sun was inching inexorably toward the western edge of the escarpment. Two hours of light left.

While Lambat gutted and caped the bushbuck, we walked back to the truck. Lesombolo looked grim. He said something whiny to Bill.

"The *mzee's* afraid that the sound of your *bunduki* will have alerted his old enemy, the elephant that ate his *mguu*—his leg—to our presence on this haunted wonderland," Bill explained. "He might be waiting for us at Nyama Yangu's cave."

"It couldn't be the same elephant, not after all these years."

"In his mind it could," Bill said. "To him this *ndovu* is immortal. It could no more die than Nyama Yangu's spirit."

It took us another hour to reach the base of the escarpment. The sky had clouded over now, and a cold wind whistled through the giant lobelias that studded the slope. Great chunks of rock, furred with gray moss, lay at the foot of the scarp, some of them bigger than houses. The skeletons of dead trees, white as bones but bearded with moss, lay like a dead army all around. A few living trees still stood and the old man hobbled toward one. A big crooked tree, a real *mzee* of a tree, with the barely legible initials carved into it, scabbed and peeling but indisputably the work of man.

"A.H.N."

Arthur Henry Neumann.

It was all coming true.

Daring us to follow him, old Lesombolo began stumping his way toward the rock face. The brim of his weathered black fedora flapped like bat wings in the wind, his tattered field jacket rippled to its gusts, his *shuka* snapped around his long black skinny, almost skeletal leg. He looked already dead, resurrected, ghostlike in the gray wind. We rounded the corner of a gigantic boulder hard against the cliff....

Maybe it was the elevation, maybe a touch of fever, maybe just nerves, but....

The elephant stood before us. Ears flared like sails in the wind. Trunk raised like a monstrous python. Massive, gray, wrinkled as the pages of time, his eyes blazing red fires that guttered in the howling wind. The old man was gone, Bill was gone, Lambat had vanished. I raised the rifle to my shoulder—suddenly realizing that it was the .458, magically materialized into my hands—and aimed for one of those flickering red eyes, terror in my heart.

I fired.

The bullet whanged off the lichen-grown rock face, throwing sparks, and ululated off through the wind....

"Bloody hell!" Bill yelled. "What are you doing, you idiot?" He was livid.

The elephant was gone. In its place stood bulbous rock and rosecolored moss, some of it as bright as the tusker's eyes I'd imagined. Terror was instantly replaced by shame.

"Uh, I—my finger must have slipped," I stuttered lamely.

"Well, now I've seen everything." Bill grabbed the rifle from my hands. "I could feel the wind from that bullet over my head. My God, Bwana, I can't take you anywhere."

The trackers were laughing. Even Lesombolo was laughing. And the wind as well.

Inside the cave we brushed away spiders, swatted angrily at bats, sensed rather than saw the quick slither of an escaping snake. We dug through moldy earth, cold and heavy, and the shovel struck sheet metal. The rotted handles of the footlockers tore away as we dragged the trunks out into the underwater light of sundown.

We opened the lids. Inside them was....

Nothing but dust. All that remained of the Treasure of Nyama Yangu was the dust of many elephants' teeth, along with a few curious stubs scrimshawed by the teeth of the rats and mice that had eaten the ivory over the course of nearly seventy years. As we stood there, nonplussed, an eddy of wind caught the ivory dust and whirled it out over the Lorogi forest, scattering it far and wide, back to the place from which it had come.

Bill started laughing, and I laughed too. Laughter is contagious and soon the Africans were laughing uproariously with us, though they had no idea why—even old Lesombolo, his wrinkled black face suddenly half a century younger. We all laughed until our faces were stiff, then laughed some more.

It started to rain.

"AWA," Bill said. "Africa Wins Again."

A whole new round of laughter....and a long drive back to camp, a long cold drive through the rain.

*Remember, man, that thou art dust, and unto dust shalt thou return.*

# Everything Your Heart Desires

IN SOME STRANGE WAY THE BIRDS we kill fly on forever. Perhaps it's the broken arc, the interrupted parabola, the high zig through the alders that never quite made it to zag—all those incompletions crying out to be consummated. But something is there that keeps them airborne if only in our hearts, their wings forever roaring at the base of our trigger fingers. The partridge that puffs to the shot string this morning at the edge of some frost-crisp apple orchard in the hills of Vermont is the self-same bird—but totally different, of course—as the very first dove we ever knocked down, a lifetime ago, over a Midwestern cornfield. And watched in disbelief the pale feathers spill slowly from a saffron sky.

Sometimes, drunk or dreaming, I see the world crisscrossed in a webwork of avian force fields, the flight paths of ghost birds winging on out as if they'd never been hit. In the end, of course, they will weave our own rough winding sheets....

The big Bedford lorries had arrived the day before, so by the time we wheeled into the campsite along the Ewaso Nyiro River, the tents were up—taut, green, smelling of hot canvas and spicy East African dust. It was a sandy country, red and tan, and the river rolled silently but strong, dark almost as blood, under a fringe of scrawny-trunked doum palms and tall, time-worn boulders. Sand rivers cut the main watercourse at right angles, and the country rolled away to the north and west in a shimmer of pale tan haze. The fire was pale and the kettle whistled a merry welcome.

This was the last camp of the month-long shooting safari through
Kenya's bone-dry Northern Frontier Province, a hunt that had begun three
weeks earlier at Naibor Keju in the Samburu country near Maralal, then
swung northward through the lands of the Rendile and Turkana tribes to
Lake Rudolf, and back down across the Chalbi and Kaisut deserts past
Marsabit Mountain to the Ewaso Nyiro.

"I call it EDB," Bill said as we climbed down out of the green Toyota
safari wagon. "Elephant Dung Beach. The first time I camped here the
lads had to shovel the piles aside before we could pitch our tents, it was
that thick. *Ndovus* everywhere."

Not anymore. On the way in from Archer's Post, Bill had pointed out
the picked skeleton of an elephant killed by poachers, and not long since,
judging by the lingering smell. We'd stopped to look it over—vertebrae
big as chopping blocks, ribs fit for a whaleboat, the broad skull still crawling with ants, and two splintered, gaping holes where the ivory had been
hacked out.

"*Shifta*," Bill said, and when we got into camp the safari crew confirmed his diagnosis. *Shifta* were even then the plague of northeastern
Kenya, raiders from neighboring Somalia who felt, perhaps with some jus-
tification, that the whole upper right-hand quadrant of Kenya rightly
belonged to them. When the colonial powers divided Africa among themselves, they all too often drew arbitrary boundaries regardless of tribal tra-
ditions. The Somalis—a handsome, fiercely Islamic people related to the
Berbers of northwest Africa and the ancient Egyptians (theirs was the
Pharaonic "Land of Punt")—are nomads for the most part, and boundaries
mean as little to them as they do to migrating wildebeest. But these
migrants, armed with Russian AKs and plastic explosives, have blood in
their eyes. They poach ivory and rhino horn, shoot up *manyattas* (villages) and police posts, mine the roads, and blow up trucks or buses with
no compunction. Sergeant Nganya, a lean old Meru in starch-stiff Empire
Builders and a faded beret, led us over to a lugga near the riverbank. In
the bottom were the charred, cracked leg bones of a giraffe, scraps of rotting hide, the remains of a cook fire, and an empty 7.62 mm shell case
stamped Cartridge, M1943—the preferred diet of the Soviet AK-47 assault
rifle. Nganya, who had been with Winter since their days together in the
Kenya game department, handed the cartridge over without a word.

"I'm sure they'll leave us alone," Bill said as we drank our *chai* under
the cool fly of the mess tent. "They know we're armed, and the lads will
keep a sharp lookout around the *kampi*. Just to ensure sweet dreams for
one and all, though, I'll post guards at night. Not to worry."

That evening we went out for buffalo. I still had one on my license, having killed a decent bull on the Tinga Plateau near Naibor Keju. He died in a splendid sunset.

Tonight's sunset was as gaudy as that one had been: a skyful of purples and mauves and lavenders shot through with ribbons of dying fire. Walking down the riverbank through those pyrotechnics was like strolling through a gallery of bad picture postcards. There were crocodiles along the bank, big ones that slithered off into the dark, fast water with a speed that belied their size; baboons yapped and snarled in the bush across the way. Big abrupt knobs of dark red rock thrust up through the trees and we scanned them as we walked, keeping our eyes skinned for *shifta*. And suddenly one was standing there—tall and skinny against the light, heart-stopping in his instant emergence from nothingness. Then I saw that it was Lambat, our head tracker, who only a minute earlier had been right behind me. He must have scampered up the hundred-foot kopje like a klipspringer.

"Ah," said Bill, following my gaze. "His Lordship's having a *shufti*—a bit of a look-see, as you'd say in America. Aha—and he sees something!"

Lambat had squatted and was peering intently upriver. It was almost too melodramatic, like a scene from a John Ford western where the intrepid Indian scout on the rimrock suddenly spots Geronimo's band. But this was real life and there was that high intensity about Lambat: slow, quiet, loose-jointed as a dead snake during times of inaction, he literally "lit up" when he spotted game, his dull dark skin suddenly glowing like polished mahogany, his muscles showing like well-wrapped cables, eyes bright as a gundog's on point. Now he raised his hands, palms forward, fingers spread. Ten. Then folded them, and opened them again.

And again and again.

"Christ," Bill said, "he sees forty, fifty—sixty or more."

"*Shifta*?"

"No." Bill laughed. "Buffalo. At least I hope that's what he means."

The herd was feeding a quarter of a mile ahead of us, along the riverbank. We could smell them before we saw them, that sweet stench of the cow barn that put me in mind of boyhoods in northern Wisconsin: trout streams and roast-chicken suppers in the big, comfortable lakeside kitchen after the evening chores were done and the herd milked, while bats flew over the flowering honeysuckle. But this was savage Africa; milkmen of doom, we bellied up to deal death to these wild bovines.

"That one on the right," Bill whispered beside me in the bush. "With his head down right now, near that group of cows; he's lifting his head up, chewing, chewing, now looking toward us. Shaking off the flies."

"I see him."

"He'll go over forty inches," Bill said. "He's the best of the lot. Hold on bone, Bwana, right on the shoulder. We want to break him him down. But don't shoot until you're ready."

"Yes."

"Are you sure you can take him?"

"Yes."

"We don't want to be going in after him now. Not in this light."

*Pa-wham!*

The bull dropped to the shot.

The herd broke and stampeded—bulls, cows, and calves erupting like a giant black mortar burst as the dead bull hit the ground.

"Oh, shit! Look at that!" Bill was beside himself with frustration. Out of the thick bush to the right stepped a bull buffalo that looked, in the dying red light, to be half again as big as the one I'd dropped. "Oh, look at that big sod! He must have been crossed with a Texas Longhorn. He's one for the book, Bwana, but we can't kill him now, can we? You've shot your limit."

The big buffalo and two smaller ones went over to the dead bull and hooked at him viciously, grunting and lowing.

"Crikey," Bill said, "aren't they bloody marvelous? Look at them, all scabby and thick and covered in shit, yet beautiful nonetheless. I've killed them in their hundreds, over the years. Yet if I had my way, I'd put them all back on their feet just to see them galloping the plains again. Knee-deep through tall, sweet grass!"

His eyes shone noonday blue in the gathering darkness.

So blood can pall. This buffalo was the last of the big, warm, dangerous animals for that safari, and we would finish out the week at EDB with bird shooting. It was a welcome relief, a slow, leisurely cooling-out from the high tension and dark tragedy of big game, and for me doubly so, since bird hunting has always been my first love among the shooting sports. But this was a different kind of bird hunting. I'd grown up on ruffed grouse, woodcock, sharptails, and pheasants in the upper Middle West, and that kind of gunning meant cold mornings, iron skies, crisp wild apples, the crunch of bright leaves under muddy boots. It was all tamaracks and muskegs, old pine slashings, glacial moraines, and ink-black ponds, the country peopled with tough little Finns and potato-faced Germans. In the one-horse logging towns, we whiled away the evenings on draft beer, bratwurst, and snooker. The great unspoken fear in that land of Green Bay Packer worship weren't *shifta* but something far more fearsome: the Chicago Bears.

The contrast between American and African bird shooting comes quickly clear. The morning after the buffalo hunt we are up before dawn. Even this coolest part of the day is tee-shirt weather; hyenas giggle down-river and a great fish eagle winnows the air overhead as we sip strong Kenyan coffee at first light. There are lion tracks outside the tents, fresh ones—great bold pug marks that circled the camp twice during the night. But our guards, the wry Turkana named Otiego and the big, slab-faced Samburu we call Red Blanket, report no signs of *shifta* during their watches. Yet they hadn't seen the lion either....

Not far from the river is a hot spring, a *maji moto* in Swahili, and we walk in quietly through a low ground fog, armed only with 20-gauge shot-guns. Soon the sand grouse will be flying. Lambat leads the way, peering intently into the mist. He raises a hand: halt. We hear a huffing sound in the fog, then dimly make out two dark bulky shapes. "*Kifaro*," hisses Lambat. "*Mama na mtoto.*"

Either the fog thins or adrenaline sharpens my vision, for suddenly they come into focus: a big female rhino and her calf. The mother whuffs again, aware that something is wrong but unable, with her weak eyes and the absence of wind, to zero in on the threat. She shakes a head horned like a Mexican saddle and shuffles off into the haze, followed by her horn-less offspring, which looks at this distance like an outsized hog. I'd often jumped deer while bird hunting in the U.S., and once a moose got up and moved out of an alder swale I was pushing for woodcock near Greenville, Maine. But rhino are somehow different. If only for the heightened puck-er factor.

The sun bulges over the horizon, a giant blood-orange, and instantly the fog is gone, sucked up by the dry heat of day. But then it seems to return, in the whistling, whizzing form of a million sand grouse, chunky birds as quick and elusive as their distant relatives, the white-winged doves and mourning doves I'd shot back home.

These are chestnut-bellied sand grouse, *Pterocles exustus*, the most common of some six species that inhabit the dry thorn scrublands of Africa. They fly to water each morning, hitting the available waterholes for about an hour soon after dawn, fluttering over the surface to land, drink, and soak up water in their throat feathers for their nestlings to drink during the dry season.

I promptly began to miss them, overwhelmed and wild-eyed at their sky-blackening abundance. Then I settled down as the awe receded and I began knocking down singles and doubles at a smart clip. It was fast, neck-wrenching shooting with the birds angling in from every direction. I stood under the cover of an umbrella acacia, surrounded by shell husks, the barrel soon hot enough to raise blisters, shooting until my shoulder grew numb. Bill stood nearby, calling the shots and laughing at my misses.

"Quick, behind you, Bwana!"

I spun around to see a pair slashing in overhead, mounted the gun with my feet still crossed, folded the lead bird, and then leaned farther back to take the trailer directly above me—*pow!* The recoil, in my unbalanced, leg-crossed stance, dropped me on my tailbone. But the bird fell too.

"Splendid," Bill said with a smirk. "Just the way they teach it at the Holland & Holland Shooting School. The Classic Twisting, Turning, High-Overhead, Passing, Fall-on-Your-Arse Double. Never seen it done better, I do declare!"

Then it was over. The sand grouse vanished as quickly as they'd appeared. The trackers began to pick up the dead and locate any "runners." There were few wounded birds. I'd been shooting sixes, the high-brass loads we'd used earlier in the safari for vulturine and helmeted guineafowl. The heavy shot killed cleanly when I connected. You could use No. 7½ shot, perhaps even eights on these lightly feathered, thin-skinned birds, and increase the bag a bit, but there is really no need to. By using heavier shot, you ensure swifter kills, and there is never a dearth of birds.

Or so I was thinking. Just then one of the birds—a cripple, far out near the white-scaled salt of the hot spring's rim—scuttled away, trailing a shattered wing. Lambat stooped like a shortstop fielding a line drive, grabbed a stone and slung it sidearm. It knocked the bird dead at twenty yards. He picked up the grouse and brought it to me, walking long and limber, dead casual, a look of near-pity on his face as he placed it in my hand. Ah, the sorry, weak *Mzungu* with his costly firestick, blasting holes in the firmament with those expensive shells, when there were rocks right there for the picking. "His Lordship," indeed.

**T**HE CAMP WAS IN AN UPROAR when we returned. *Shifta*—four of them, scruffy little men with dirty shirts and heads wrapped in towels, accompanied by even scruffier dogs—had approached the camp. Ganya had driven them away with warning rifle-fire. No, they hadn't shot back, merely eased themselves into cover and out of range. They had faded southward, into the tangled vegetation of the riverbank. Everyone was excited. Even the old *mpishi*—the safari cook—was muttering and shaking his head as he poked at his perpetual fire. Normally the *mpishi* was Mister Cool.

After a lunch of oxtail soup, courtesy of the previous day's buffalo, and grilled sand grouse breasts, we drove up the river to Merti, the last town before the Ewaso Nyiro makes its great bend and loses itself in the wastes of the Lorian Swamp, hard by the Hothori and Sabena deserts. There is a police post at Merti and Bill wanted check in, letting them know we were in the area. Along the way I kept seeing wrecked vehicles beside the twisting, twin-rutted road—fully half a dozen of them in the course of a thirty-mile drive. Some were badly rusted and nearly buried with wind-blown sand, but others seemed more recent. We stopped to examine one. The frame was bent like a steel pretzel, the hood ripped as if by a giant can opener. Even the wheel rims were twisted. The vehicle was barely recognizable as a Land Rover. But what could have torn the truck up so badly? On this barely traveled road, it could hardly have been a multi-truck collision.

*"Plastique,"* said Bill. "C-4 or the Russian or Egyptian equivalent. A land mine did this work—the *shifta* use them all over the NFD."

Command-detonated?

"I doubt it. Probably a simple contact fuse. They don't use vehicles themselves as a rule, so why should they wait around to blow up a specific target when they can just plant a mine in a busy road and go about their business? They don't seem to care who they blow up. Whoever comes along will be a Kenyan or a tourist."

Merti, when we got there, had the look and feel of a besieged "strategic hamlet" in Vietnam. The police post was encircled ten feet high with barbed wire, its corners guarded by machine-gun towers. The town itself resembled the old, grainy sepiatone photographs of laagers during the Boer War, and you almost expected to see wide-hatted, leathery voortrekkers hung with bandoliers lounging outside the *duka* drinking beer, waiting for the order from Smuts or Botha that would send their commando back into the field. But the Kenya police were definitely on the defensive in this undeclared war.

"Oh yes indeed, sir," the sergeant in charge said, smiling widely. "There are *shifta* about. Perhaps a hundred of them. Bad men, yes. *Mbaya sana."* But he wasn't doing anything about them. And rightly so, Bill pointed out later. If he sortied from the town, the *shifta* might lure him and his men deeper into the waterless thorn-scrub while others swung back to loot the *dukas* in town and make off with whatever supplies and weapons they could lay their hands on.

"Well," Bill told him, "we're upriver in Block Seven near Kittermaster's Camp, hunting, and I'm sure they won't bother us."

"Oh no, sir." The sergeant smiled. "Of course not. Not with the police so close at hand." They both laughed heartily.

We stopped at the *duka* and drank a warm Tusker beer. The dusty, cool shop was pleasant but poorly stocked.

"I came off safari once, years ago, into a little *duka* like this," Bill recalled. "Back in my Anti-Stock-Theft days with the Kenya constabulary. I'd been chasing Turkana cattle thieves all over hell and gone. God, it was hot. What I wanted more than anything was a good, clean shave, and I'd run out of razor blades days earlier. I came into the *duka* and asked the owner what he had in stock. A big, happy, smiling chap he was, like that police sergeant we were talking to just now. 'Oh, Bwana,' he said, 'we have everything your heart desires!' He gestured around at his shelves. 'By chance would you have a razor blade?' I asked him.

"'*Hakuna*,' quoth he rather sadly. 'I have none.'"

Bill laughed.

"'Everything your heart desires.' Don't you love it, Bwana?"

In the evenings I was reading myself to sleep with a book from Bill's copious collection of Africana: a 1910 edition of a book titled *In the Grip of the Nyika*, by Lieutenant Colonel J.H. Patterson, D.S.O. The colonel had made his name by killing a pair of voracious lions that had stopped the construction of the Mombasa–to–Uganda railway in the early years of this century by killing and devouring scores of Indian coolies who were laying the track. Patterson recounted those adventures in a best-selling book called *The Man-Eaters of Tsavo*.

This later volume, which Bill inevitably called *In the Grip of the Knickers*, is about a safari Patterson made along the Ewaso Nyiro, surveying the boundaries of the Northern Frontier District in company with an old school chum of his, fresh out from England, whom he identifies only as "B." Accompanying them is B.'s newlywed bride, a comely young Englishwoman called "Mrs. B."

Near the place where we were now camped, "B." had allegedly fallen ill with fever and one evening, without warning, blown his brains out with a pistol. Patterson buried his friend, consoled the grieving widow, and got on with his survey. Later the colonel himself came down with fever and was nursed back from the brink of death by the brave Mrs.B.,whom he later married.

"Makes you wonder, doesn't it?" Bill would say. "Maybe there was a little slap–and–tickle going on between the handsome White Hunter and his brave, lovely little Clientess—it's been known to happen, Bwana. Picture the scene. Poor old B. wakes up sweating beneath his mozzie net, out of his head with fever. His wife is nowhere to be seen. The dank heat of the African night, lions coughing, hyenas cackling in the dark, and suddenly a girlish giggle from the White Hunter's tent—that sort of thing.... Then, a shot rings out! 'The Short Happy Life of Francis Macomber' in embryo, wouldn't you say?"

But the book was fascinating and I would slope off into dreams of blood and illicit love, hearing the hyenas whoop, the crunch of their jaws on fragile bone, and see looming up through the river mists the vague menacing shape of.... Abdul the Abominable, the Power *Shifta*. He'd be lying there in ambush for us, to pay us for our sins. Never mind that the sins were undefined, we all had plenty to our name. Images of slow, bright knives, staked out covered with honey in the track of the *siafi,* the safari ants. Abdul standing there in the dark, cackling at our helplessness like a foul-breathed, rot-eating *fisi....*

"**I** THINK I'LL GO OUT THIS AFTERNOON with the shotgun," I told Bill at lunch on our last day at E.D.B. "A rough shoot—see what I can walk up. There must be plenty of birds right around camp."

"Sounds like a fine idea," Bill said. "I've got to stay here and organize the packing, though. You can take Lambat and Otiego along with you to push the birds up. There's no end of *ndeges* around here. I hear them calling in the morning—guinea fowl, francolin, yellow-necked spur fowl, maybe even some button quail. You'll have a good time, I'm sure. *Ndeges mingi sana* hereabouts, birds galore."

And *shifta* as well, but we left that unspoken. It was too beautiful a day to worry about them, at least out loud. This was my last day afield, and the bird shooting so far had been an alien form—there'd been the sand grouse, of course, and I'd shot driven guinea fowl with Bill once, on an old coffee shamba that had previously belonged to Karen Blixen, a.k.a. Isak Dinesen, the *Out of Africa* woman, and it had been good shooting but too formal, too much like an English driven pheasant shoot for my rough-and-ready American taste. The boys had formed a line at the top of a long, brushy slope and pushed the birds down to us where we stood above the jungly banks of the Tana River near where it rises beyond Thika, the guineas lurching into the air well above us, big dark birds heavier than pheasants but just as fast as they poured past, cackling, and we shot fast and furious, folding some nicely but seeing others slant down, heavy-hit, legs trailing, to land in the riverside tangle. When we went in to finish them, we found fresh buffalo sign: steaming mounds of shiny dung, trampled shrubbery.

"What do we do if they come?" I asked Bill, hefting the 20-gauge pitifully in my hands.

"Climb," Bill laughed. "*Panda juu.* There are plenty of trees at hand."

"I don't know if I'm still that arboreal," I said doubtfully.

"You will be, Bwana," he said. "Don't worry about it. Nature will take its course. I was in a situation like this with a fat old English nobleman once. He scampered up a thorn tree like a bloody *nugu*—just as agile as a monkey. Never even let out a yelp from the thorn stabs. Didn't feel them."

We'd gone in then and collected our birds, and the buff left us alone. Just as the *shifta* would leave me alone today. I hoped.

Yet deep down it was because of the *shifta*—the chance of them being there—that I wanted to do this. Every bird hunter knows the neck-itching feeling that crawls up from your kidneys when you walk into a good cover. As if something deadly were waiting there, silent in the mottled green dark. What's waiting, though, is no deadlier than humiliation if you blow the shot. Yet when the bird gets up with a rattle and a roar, it's as if some bogey man suddenly sprang out at you, heart-stopping, remorseless, Abdul the Objectionable in his final, fatal pounce. The adrenaline rush is beyond comparison. This would be even better.

The country upstream from camp was thick with wait-a-bit thorn and elephant grass, tough going as we pushed into it. Behind us the sounds of camp life—clanking pots, happy conversation in English and Swahili— quickly faded; ahead the doum palms and borassus swayed, their shadows shifting black on the bright grass. A heavy silence, broken only by the buzz of flies and bees, the rusty creak of nooning birds.

Otiego swung wide to the right and slapped his spear at the edge of a low thorn thicket. A bird got up with the forever-startling feathery whirr—a long brown bird, big as a pheasant—and I centered it, *pow!* Then another, and three more. I didn't hear my second barrel fire, but there were two birds down. Feathers still falling through the hot, hard light. Otiego brought them back—yellow-necked spur fowl, their throats pale orange, conspicuously bare, the wet dead eyes rimmed with bare skin, pebbly red.

We could hear others ahead of us calling back and forth, *graark, grak, grak*. They ran ahead of us as we approached, we could see them scuttling gray-brown through the scrub. Then from the left a different bird got up—darker, chunkier—and Lambat fell flat as he he saw me swing past him, then shoot. The bird fell down. Its white throat and legs and mottled belly proclaimed it a Shelley's francolin, counterpart of the sharp-tailed grouse of my boyhood.

In the denser forest back of the riverbank, another variety abounded—Heuglin's francolin, dark-feathered and plump as a European partridge. They got up like ruffed grouse, with a great spooking thunder of wings in there under the confining forest canopy and had the same maddening habit of waiting until you were past, then lining out with a tree trunk between them and the gun barrel.

In the open, with the pheasant-like spur fowl and the tight-holding, sharptail-like Shelley's francolin, I couldn't seem to miss; now it was hard to score a hit. Otiego grinned wickedly and clucked his mock disapproval.

Back out in the open, we jumped a small covey of buff-colored, round-winged birds that buzzed off like outsized bumblebees. Button quail. I dropped two before they pitched in less than a hundred yards ahead. Lambat scooped them up on the run, but when we got to where the singles landed we couldn't trigger a single reflush. Yet there had been at least eight in the covey, perhaps ten—slow fliers at best—that landed in the tall grass. We could hear them scuttling, hear their frog-like *whoo-whoo-whoo* as they ran. We didn't see them again. The dead birds in hand looked vaguely like quail, but there was something odd about their feet. Then I noticed that they lacked the hind toes of true quail. It certainly didn't seem to hinder their speed on the ground.

For three hours we zigzagged through that wild, thorn-fanged riverside bush, a game-bird heaven, the trackers working like clever gundogs, spotting each possible hiding place, circling beyond it, then pushing through to put the birds out toward the gun. On some I shot nicely, on others I might as well have thrown the shotgun at them. But it was a Time Machine—no, a Time-and-Place Machine. At one moment I was back in a southern Wisconsin pheasant field, swinging on a fast-moving rooster with the corn tassels crunching underfoot; in the next I was kicking the soybean stubble for Georgia quail. Then I was up in Minnesota working the shortgrass prairie for sharptails, and in the next step jumping a partridge out of alder edges in Maine.

Yet at the same time I was aware that this was Africa: There could be a surly old bull buffalo just under the bank to my left, very angry at having his midday snooze disrupted; or a lion behind the next bush, sleeping off his midnight gluttony but not too lazy to get up and chomp a clumsy *mzungu*. And above all, there was Abdul & Company, with automatic rifles, plastic land mines, and a total lack of compunction when it came to killing unwary travelers.

By the time we swung back into camp, Lambat and Otiego each had ten birds dangling from their hands and I a few brace more slapping my hip, their heads forced through my belt loops, their shot-loosened feathers sticking to my legs with a glue of dried blood, both theirs and mine, thanks to the thorns. The three of us were laughing as we came out of the *nyika*.

Bill was sitting outside the mess tent, having his afternoon tea. He looked up with a quizzical smile. "Did you have a decent shoot, Bwana?"

"It was everything my heart desired."

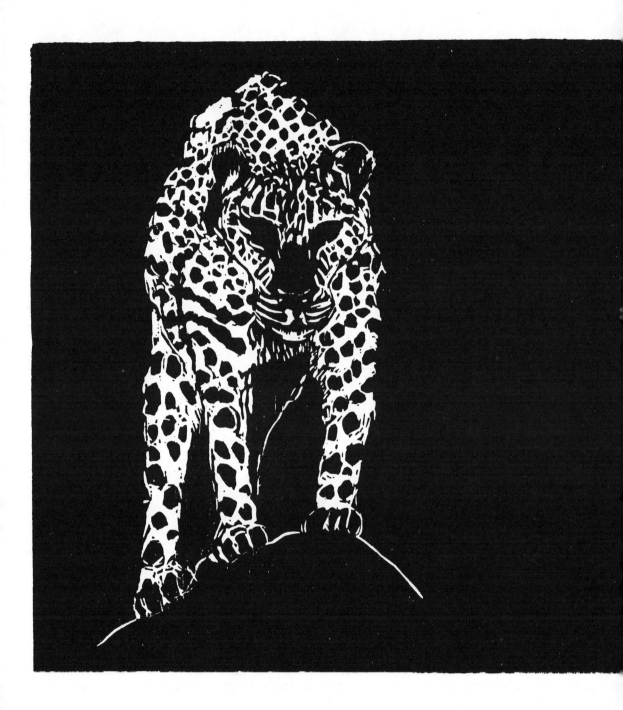

# The Leopard of Lorian Swamp

*And slowly answered Arthur from the barge:*
*The old order changeth, yielding place to new,*
*And God fulfills himself in many ways,*
*Lest one good custom should corrupt the world.*
     —Tennyson, *Idylls of the King*

**W**E HAD JUST FINISHED A MEMORABLE safari in the Northern Frontier District of Kenya, one on which I had taken, in the eleventh hour of the final day, a very fine leopard. It was my first. A male, it pegged out at nearly eight feet from nose to tail tip, and we were celebrating the kill, relaxing at Bill Winter's home in Nanyuki before my imminent departure Stateside. It was a Sunday afternoon, cool and cloudy on the slopes of Mount Kenya. We decided to run down to the Sportsman's Arms for tea. A British regimental band held forth on the hotel grounds that lazy evening, and we took our tea on the veranda to the strains of "The Colonel Bogey March."

You know the tune, but if not, perhaps the words often sung to it will bring back the melody.

"It's horseshit—that makes the grass grow green...."

I sang them *sotto voce* between sips of piping-hot Darjeeling.

"Look at that old gent, Bwana," Bill whispered after swallowing a bite of lemon tart. He cast his eyes briefly to my left. Seated near us at a wickerwork garden table, one gouty foot propped on a chair as he beat time to the music, was a splendid wreck of a fellow, mottled of cheek but bright of eye, with a hoary set of sidewhiskers and a magnificent if somewhat drinksodden moustache. He sipped at a rust-colored gin and bitters, no ice.

"Sir George McArthur Ponsonby, V.C." Bill said. "A grand old ruin, hey? But he was a *dume* in his day, a real bull. Won the Victoria Cross at Passchendaele in the Great War, marched on Waziristan with General Climo in 1919, exemplary Colonial service, both military and civilian, in Nyasaland, the Cameroons, and Tanganyika, a veteran of safaris *mingi sana*—many, many great hunts—back in the days when the word meant something, when they went in on foot, with porters balancing the loads on their heads. He can tell you a tale or two, old Sir George. What say we ask him over for a drink and a bit of a chin-wag?"

We did, and in due course Bill told Sir George about my leopard.

"Wasn't by chance wearing gold ankle bracelets, was it?" Sir George asked when I finished my modest story. "Graven with mystical writing?"

"No, sir," I answered, puzzled. Bill was grinning behind his hand. "Should it have been?"

Sir George chuckled and assured me most definitely that it should not have been. Not if I valued my health and sanity.

Bill winked, then tugged his left earlobe, a signal advising me to activate the small tape recorder I carried, locked and loaded, in the breast pocket of my bush vest.

Sir George ordered another gin-and-bitters. When it arrived, he proceeded to relate a tale of his own concerning leopards, the tale of a strange and dreadful hunt. It had occurred nearly half a century earlier, in the same reaches of the NFD from which we had just returned. Some years ago, he began, in the early 1920s, he and another Englishman were hunting along the Ewaso Nyiro River, slowly following its sinuous route through that great game country to where it hemorrhage finally, as so many African rivers do, into the sands of an ever-expanding desert, leaving only a fetid marsh to punctuate its finish. Here then is his tale, abridged only slightly so as not to offend what is blithely termed a "family" readership....

**I**N THE COURSE OF OUR TREK down the 'Washo,' we happened upon a small *manyatta*—a village of shabby grass huts—on the edge of the Lorian Swamp, where that great blood-red river ends its career. The inhabitants, a degenerate breed of Marsh 'Dorobos, had never seen white men before. They fled weeping at the approach of our safari. Our porters, feeling superior to these rude savages, laughed long and hard at them, making jests in raucous Kiswahili that accused the poor savages of such bestial sins as snake worship and intimate congress with hyenas.

"The naked bums of these dusky Adams and Eves had no sooner vanished into the nettles than our lads began looting. We had already discovered, to our mutual dismay, that there was no controlling these boisterous hirelings once theft was in prospect, short of shooting a few of them. Twice thus far we'd been forced to do so, and both of us feared that yet another such episode would precipitate a full-scale mutiny. Our ammunition was running low. We might not be able to quell a concerted uprising without burning the rest of it, at which point our own lives would be forfeit. And even if we slew enough of the obstreperous rascals to bring the remainder to their senses, would the survivors fulfill their duties to us the rest of the way to the Coast, or decamp in the dark of moon with all they could pilfer?

"What to do, what to do.... My companion must have perceived my indecision. He smiled coolly.

"'Heigh-ho,' said Rawley. 'I don't know about you, Sir George, but I fear my heart's all a-twitter.'

"The ball was now clearly in my court.

"'By my troth, I care not,' quoth I, with what I hoped was an insouciance equal to the moment, 'we owe God a swoon, and let it go which way it will, he who swoons this year is quit for the next.'

"Rawley punched me lightly on the shoulder. '*Pukka sahib,*' said he.

"At that point, Kabiza, our burly headman, emerged from a squalid hut with a woman in tow. He crowed lustily. The other lads gathered round in eager anticipation. It was the old story. Nothing better enlivens a friendly afternoon of looting than a spot of jiggery-pokery! Though our gang would have been content with a withered old crone, this woman was young, nubile, and to some tastes, I reckon, quite lovely to gaze upon.

"She had something of the look of a Somali about her, a tall, lissome, coffee-colored wench with the poignant overbite and wide-set, almond eyes peculiar to Hamitic women. The women you see in those Ancient Egyptian murals at the Victoria & Albert, you know, or among the Berbers and Tuaregs of contemporary Saharan Africa.

"Oddly enough, she didn't seem frightened, though she must have known how these sessions inevitably end. One of the bullies, his passion and interest spent, brains his sobbing victim with a disdainful swing of his knob-kerri. Yet she stood there in the mud, the late, low sunlight mottling her golden skin, and smiled inscrutably into the distance.

"An innocent young savage, you ask?

"I wondered myself, even then. A brace of delicate, artfully wrought ornaments, forged from some precious metal, encircled her trim ankles, touches of a higher, perhaps forgotten culture. The anklets winked in the day's red decline. The girl's cat-like eyes impressed me as well, empty as they were of any recognizable human emotion. They had a classic, almost Pharaonic look to them, as if they had been carved from antediluvian amber and buried for centuries in some great king's tomb. Then she yawned, quite prettily it seemed to me, and turned to Kabiza with a playful smile.

"That worthy threw her to the ground, cast aside his *shuka*, the toga-like garb of the country, and with a low growl proceeded to cover her. The girl drew back her knees, whether in repulsion or acceptance of her fate, I know not. Kabiza's rowdy cohorts cheered. He thrust home....

"I averted my eyes in shame, then looked back suddenly as a hideous, soul-chilling cry split the air."

He paused to sip his gin-and-bitters.

"Who was it?" I asked.

"Kabiza, of course," he said, smiling wetly. "The headman's hips seemed to buck upward for an instant. He rolled to one side, on his back. His entrails spilled forth onto the mud in a welter of gore. His eyes bulged horribly, the scarred, ape-like face contorted in pain, his fingers clutching spasmodically at his innards as he tried vainly to replace them within his gaping abdomen. And Kabiza of course, disemboweled, who shuddered and died a few moments later."

Again Sir George paused for refreshment.

"And then?"

He smiled once more.

"The girl was gone!" Sir George said triumphantly. "We stood dumbfounded. 'My God!' Rawley suddenly cried. 'Look, there!' He pointed toward a narrow alleyway that led between the huts into the depths of the swamp. I saw the thing for only an instant—the sleek, sinuous form of a leopard, its hind paws and white-furred underbelly spattered with blood, disappearing swiftly into the man-high marsh grass. Or so it seemed."

"We sat long and late at the campfire that night. Rawley had broken out the medicinal brandy—Napoleon, 1813 if I'm not mistaken—and we slugged it back as if it were hock. Our rifles stood leaning against our camp chairs. The firelight played eerily on Rawley's manly features, aging him to a seamed simulacrum of himself, a feeble octogenarian if you will.

"Major Alistair Frederic Rawley-DePuis, D.S.O., V.C., late of Her Majesty's Coldstream Guards, was no stranger to the arcana of the African bush. Seconded at his own request to the King's African Rifles at the end of the Boer War, he had battled Kikuyu, Turkana, Suk, and Nandi spearmen from Kirinyaga to the Nyandarua, from Lake Rudolph to the Kisii Plateau. By his own modest count, he had slain full three score or more of these swarthy adversaries, all of them in single combat. 'It's amazing,' he told me once, a sweet smile playing about his lips, 'how easily a bayonet slips into a man, and how difficult it is to withdraw.'

"He had fatally pistoled a laibon of the Kavirondo nation at point-blank range during a nefarious native ambush, wrestled a rungu from a crazed Maasai *moran* and killed him with his own warclub, been hexed by a Turkana witch whose potion of spider venom and euphorbia sap had been slipped unbeknownst to him into his sundowner by a turncoat batman, survived countless life-threatening episodes of African mayhem and intrigue. After seventeen years of service on the Dark Continent, though, his good Dorsetshire common sense had been subtly altered. He had begun to believe in The Darkness.

"'She's a Leopard Woman,' he said now. 'No doubt of it, Sir George.'

"'Oh, I say, old son,' I could not help but splutter. 'Isn't that putting, er... just a touch too much credence in the arcane?'

"'Not at all,' he replied. 'Though I've never come across it myself, the literature teems with eyewitness reports of such phenomena. Many of these African witchwomen have the power, one way or t'other, to change themselves at will into leopards or hyenas or aardwolves, even puff adders or mambas if they so choose, or so at least I've read. An old messmate of mine, Colonel Sidney Cartwright-Graham, reports witnessing just such a transmogrification in his book, *Nightdrums & Devilry in Danakil Land*. Chapter XIII, I believe. And Professor Woolworthy, the Cambridge myth wallah, devotes three whole chapters to the phenomenon, citing numerous examples in one or another of his swotty tomes—*Black Rites on the Blue Nile*, if I'm not mistaken.'

"'But might there not be a simpler explanation?' I asked. 'The girl could have had a knife secreted about her person, and when Kabiza jumped aboard she gralloched him.'

"'You saw the leopard as clearly as I,' Rawley replied. 'Where did it come from, and in broad daylight to boot?'

"He had a point, of course. Yet the eyes have a way of playing tricks on the forebrain, particularly at moments of sudden stress, when confusion reigns and events transpire too swiftly. The African bush, as I'm sure you chaps are well aware, provides an all-too-fertile ground for the sensitive European imagination. Fantasy runs riot.

"'Well, at least the incident seems to have put a quietus to the porters' mischief,' I said. 'I noticed them just now replacing their il-lgotten goods, all of them meek as lambs.'

"We decided to break camp at first light the following morning. The sooner we were clear of this unholy ground, the better. Another five days of long marches through the Hothori and Sabena Deserts should find us on the verdant banks of the Tana River, where we could hire new porters and continue our hunt in a more leisurely fashion, downriver toward Lamu and the Coast.

"The boys built a tall, strong *zareeba* of thornbush around the *manyatta*, fueled up their fires, and wrapped themselves uneasily in their blankets for the night. We too retired. About three hours later, Rawley and I were awakened by screams and shouts. Snatching our rifles, we leaped out of the tent clad only in our *kikois*. Total confusion reigned. Finally we were able to learn that the leopardess had returned, grabbed Achmed, one of our likeliest lads, between her jaws, then quick as a wink bounded clean over the top of the *zareeba*, back into that awful darkness. We could hear the poor boy screaming and bewailing his fate, the sound fading slowly into the depths of the morass. Then through the dark came an audible crunch, followed by silence. Rawley and I sat up the rest of the night, our rifles across our knees, but she did not return. No, no....

"No, she saved that for the morrow."

Sir George finished his gin-and-bitters, ordered another from the comely Meru waitress hovering nearby with her tray, then continued.

"We were up before dawn, the boys gladly shouldering their heavy loads, our meager, dwindling supplies as well as an abundance of horns, hides, and no small weight of ivory, for Rawley had slain a *tembo* whose tusks weighed more than 140 pounds each, and I one only marginally less toothy. Shunning a proper breakfast, we wolfed down a few pieces of biltong on the march.

"We gave the Lorian Swamp a wide berth as we skirted it, heading south by southeast for the Tana. Toward noon, just as we neared the end of the savannah, with the supposed safety of open desert visible dead ahead, the leopardess struck again. Creeping up through the tall grass, she nabbed the last porter in the long line. Nabbed him by the throat this time, so that he could utter no more than a muffled shriek before she disappeared back into the waving grass, with him dangling crosswise in her jaws. Once more we were treated to the sound of The Queen of Darkness at table, harsh purrs of contentment emanating from her throughout her repast.

"We hurried on. Ironically enough, the Sabena desert, one of the fiercest in the world, offered us our only hope of succor. Not even a spring hare could hide on its barren surface, much less a large, spotted cat, no matter how stealthy her approach. The pitiless sun, which dried us like so many pieces of that very biltong wherewith we had broken our fast, at the same time illumined everything under its gaze. We counted on it to highlight the leopardess, granting us at least enough law to get off a shot or two—from my 'best' gun, a .450 Rigby Nitro Express double rifle, or Rawley's .303 Lee-Enfield. Ah, but Old Sol let us down, that he did.

"At midafternoon, she appeared out of nowhere—perhaps a small, unnoticed depression in the otherwise flat ground. She disemboweled two more porters with quick paw slashes, leaving her just time enough, before we came up, to peel away their faces with her remorseless jaws. This time we did not pause to bury the bodies.

"All day it went that way, and the next day, and the one after that. Our route across that ghastly wasteland was marked, and perhaps still is, with the bones of our dead. And with the loads they were carrying. Many fine trophies went to waste out there, eaten no doubt by jackals and hyenas.

"We tried, for the first few evenings, sitting up over the corpses of the newly slain in hopes of a shot at this demon leopardess. But she was too clever for us. While Rawley looked one way and I the other, she crept into camp unbeknownst and murdered a few more of our gibbering porters.

"Finally Rawley had had enough. 'The next time she strikes,' said he, 'I'm going after her.'

"'But, man!' I remonstrated. 'That's just what she wants. She'll do for you, mark my words!' All the rational explanations I had held of Kabiza's death had long since evaporated in the desert's dry air, in the unmitigated terror of that awful, endless trek. 'She's uncanny,' I cried, 'unkillable, the Devil herself, incarnate!'

"He smiled, rather sadly, I thought. As if he were resigned.

"'I cannot sit idly by for one more hour without doing something,' he calmly replied. He picked up his Lee-Enfield and checked its fittings, tightening an action screw here, a sling swivel there, then applying a thin coat of gun oil to the parts he felt required it. Lastly he scrutinized his soft-point bullets for deformities, to ensure against jams. It was a work-worn weapon, that Enfield. It had seen service in South Africa, France, India, and Africa, from Cairo to Capetown. It had dispatched more big game and more enemies of the Crown than any other dozen of its kind. Now it would pit its pluck, its English mettle (if you'll pardon the pun) against the dark, daft power of the Supernatural....

"Just then came an all-too-familiar scream and gurgle, trailing off into the night. Without a moment's hesitation, Rawley plunged into the gloom."

Sir George stopped. The regimental band had packed up its instruments and long since departed. Night had fallen, and with it a sharp, bone-biting chill. The old gentleman peered about, then shivered.

"Perhaps we'd best resume our conversation at a later date," he said. "It's getting a bit parky for these old bones."

"No, no, Sir George!" I said, nearly babbling. "I'm leaving for America in the morning, don't know when I'll be back again. Why don't you come inside and join us for supper? Be our guest. It would give me great pleasure."

"Hmm," he said doubtfully, knowing full well that he had his hook firmly planted in the corner of my mouth, through and through. The tippet would never part. "Perhaps just a small bite of something, a modest Ploughman's Lunch, no more, but in from the cold, at any rate."

It seemed to take forever, what with our moving inside, waiting for a table to be readied, Sir George making a long overdue visit to the loo, then ordering drinks and dinner. But finally he was settled.

"Where was I?"

"Rawley had just plunged...."

"Yes, yes—into the gloom. I sat there alone for a minute, maybe more. Then my suddenly aroused sense of shame at being thought a coward propelled me after him. I pushed through the *zareeba* into the chill desert night. Rawley was nowhere to be seen, not even as my eyes adjusted to the dark. Nor could I hear him. Or anything, for that matter, save some jackals yipping far away, off in the back of beyond. I walked cautiously forward, the loaded Rigby at high port arms, my thumb on the safety for a quick shot, rather as if I were on a rough shoot for suddenly springing red partridge.

"Off to my left I could see the dark line of a *nullah*—a coulee or gulch, I believe you Yanks call it. Somehow I was instantly, perhaps instinctively, certain that the final act of this ghastly tragedy would unfold right there. I walked toward it with mounting trepidation. As I neared the edge, I heard a low whistle. It was Rawley, crouched in the lee of a boulder. I crouched low and made for him.

"'She's down there,' he whispered. 'Eating our man, the good Baraka. You can hear her at it.' I listened. I could. 'But you must return to camp, Sir George. This is my job, by rights. I invited you on this safari, and thus I am in command here.'

"'Tommyrot,' I answered. 'I outrank you ten ways from Sunday. The King says so. Now what shall we do?'

"His smile brightened the night. 'Good show,' he murmured. 'All you must do is cover me. I will work my way down to that next boulder, from which I should be able to see her. When I shoot, you must be alert to movement in any direction. She may flee at the shot, if I miss her, even if I hit her for that matter. Or she will charge. And leopards, as you well know, especially supernatural ones, are chargers. Stop her if she comes for me. Understood?'

"I nodded, and Rawley began to inch his way down the steep wall of the *nullah*, taking infinite pains not to disturb a single one of the many small boulders and stones that littered its tilting surface. The rattle of even a pebble would set off the leopard's fuse, causing her to explode in one direction or another. What felt like hours ticked past, lifetimes— spots crawled before my eyes—but finally he was in place. He looked back up the slope at me, raised his thumb, then slowly raised the Enfield...."

At that moment a steward arrived at our table with Sir George's entree. It was a smoking platter of *langouste*, flown up to Nanyuki at great expense from Malindi on the Coast. With the lobster came a bowl of melted butter, a tray of capers and sliced lemon, a mammoth serving of rice, veggies, and pickles, and an iced magnum of champagne, Moet & Chandon "Dom Perignon," no less. Some Ploughman's Lunch. Bill and I were having bangers and mash.

"Enjoy," I said, with a touch of acerbity. "But please go on with your story. And don't hesitate to talk with your mouth full."

Sir George laughed.

"*Bang!*" he said.

"What?"

"*Bang!* Rawley fired at the leopard. I saw the long gout of flame from the Enfield's muzzle and perhaps it blinded me for an instant. All hell broke loose, as they say. A loud, high-pitched pantherine shriek. The clatter of violently disturbed rocks. A long swift dark shape momentarily eclipsed the stars above Rawley's boulder. Then his sudden, anguished cry of rage.... All this in a heartbeat. The leopard had him, and he had her. I saw them for an instant, standing and swaying together like lovers, the leopard clutched in Rawley's strong embrace, her hind claws working at his abdomen. But of course I couldn't shoot for fear of hitting him. Then they toppled down into the *nullah*. I ran over to the edge and peered down, rifle at my shoulder.

"There she was—an elongate streak heading up the far side of the declivity. I swung with her and fired...."

The fork that Sir George had laden with lobster, rice, and a tidbit of stewed tomato and held, poised at mouth-level, throughout this discourse, now disappeared into his maw. He chewed thirty times, maybe more, then finally swallowed. He muffled a belch behind his napkin.

"And....?"

"Where was I?"

"The shot, you'd just fired the Rigby...."

"Yes, a right and a left, bang-bang, like two shots run together. The recoil and muzzle flash prevented me from seeing if either shot had told. I heard no scrabbling in the rocks, as from a moribund animal. Nor a single cry from Rawley, not even a low moan. He was dead when I found him, poor chap. Disemboweled as completely as Kabiza. I dragged him back to camp by myself, the lads refusing to come beyond the *zareeba* until it became light. I sat by his body, waiting for dawn, thinking sad thoughts of Empire, and of the men who built it. They were heroes, all of them. Where is their like today?"

"And the leopard? What happened to her?"

"Never found her," Sir George said with a cryptic grin. "Pug marks galore down in the nullah, but no blood, no hair, no scuff marks on the bare rock. I did find something, though."

"What was it?"

"These," he said, reaching into the pocket of his frayed bush jacket. The wrinkled old paw, covered with liver spots, trembled, then unclenched, palm up. In Sir George's hand lay two well-worn golden anklets, graven with strange runes or cuneiforms. They looked ancient— far older even than this husk of a man who sat before me, smiling gently but quizzically into my soul.

Old beyond time itself....

"The lads and I found these on the dessicated body of an aged woman, who lay near a boulder at the top of the nullah. Just about in line with my shots. She had been there a long, long time, mummified by the sun and the hot, arid winds so that her corpse was light as a feather. God knows why the vultures and jackals hadn't found her, or at least the driver ants. Her leathery body was clad in skins, dry as parchment now."

We sat in silence as Sir George finished his lobster. He stretched finally, yawned behind his hand, shot a cuff and looked at his wristwatch. It was a fine old timepiece, perhaps a Patek Phillipe, but its leather band had been mended near the buckle with duct tape. "Well," he said, "you lads will have to finish the champers. No heeltaps, mind you! I'm afraid I must toddle off to slumberland. Young children and old men, they both require an early bedtime. You two young stalwarts will learn the truth of that maxim, all in the fullness of time." He rose and smiled down at us, leaning his dropsical belly against the chair top.

"Thank you for my supper," he said, "not to mention the liquid refreshment. And pleasant dreams, both of you."

SIR GEORGE'S TALE HAD MADE MY OWN leopard, killed from a blind as most are nowadays, appear rather hum-drum. All I could remember of the hunt now was the interminable waiting, the insect bites, the yearning for a smoke, the leopard's sudden appearance, as if from thin air, and then the shot that killed him. He dropped without a sound, stone dead to one touch of the trigger, one soft-pointed nip from the .375 H&H Magnum. Talk about anticlimax. Rather like modern life, really: hurry up and wait, then wait some more. Just about the time you're totally bored, bang, it's over.

"What do you make of it?" I asked Bill when the old man was gone.

He laughed and shook his head.

"This is Africa, Bwana," he said at last. "Anything can happen. But whatever the truth of the matter, it makes a nice bedtime story, doesn't it?"

# PART THREE

# THREE

# DJINNS

*The Coast is plagued by* djinns.

*Driving up to Mombasa from Shimoni, where we'd been fishing, we picked up a* mzee *who needed a lift. The road wound through cashew plantations growing dense with their dark green, waxy leaves clear out to the road and the clusters of nuts shining in the shadows. Approaching the resorts of Diani, the road ran closer to the ocean. A stiff breeze blew in through the gaps in the trees, and I rolled the window all the way down to enjoy it.*

*The old man looked out past the dunes to the blue and white water where mud banks shoaled up dark under rolling combers.*

*"There are* djinns *out there," he said. "Little men with hooked noses and big bellies who live in the mud. They are that word, 'invisible.' They try to lure you into the mud. All the evil in the world comes from those mud banks."*

*He looked around to make sure no one else was listening.*

*"They have rockets!" the old man whispered....*

*A few days later, on the beach at Watamu, Bill happened to meet a Kikuyu who'd once worked for him in his days with the Game Department. Most of the former game scout's upper teeth were missing. They'd been knocked out by a charging buffalo.*

*"What news?" Bill asked.*

*"Mbaya," the man said. "Bad. It's too expensive here on the Coast."*

*"How's that?"*

*"It's all these bloody* djinns *in the ocean. Every day my wife tells me something else they've done—another evil. On Monday the* djinns *broke the cookpot. I must buy a new one, and a chicken to sacrifice to the* djinns. *On Tuesday they burned the baby in the cookfire. Now I must not only buy medicines and salves and pay for a visit to the doctor, but this time two chickens for sacrifice. On Wednesday another* djinn *makes her breasts to ache. I must buy a goat this time—a real sacrifice. But a* mbuzi *is expensive, as you well know. Sometimes I can afford only a* kuku, *a chicken."*

*Bill said, "There seem to be plenty of* kukus *about."*

*"Ndio—yes." The game scout shook his head wearily and spat through his missing teeth. "But they are too expensive, Bwana."*

*"The* djinns *see to that," Bill agreed.*

# Slip-Slidin' Away

**W**E CAME DOWN THE ROAD toward the Masai Mara and Bill, who was driving, pointed out some hills to the northwest. "Those are the Whistling Rocks," he said. "That's where I got plugged."

We'd left Nanyuki in the early morning, winding west down Mount Kenya and then south through open savannah. Whydah birds flapped awkwardly over the grass, struggling against the drag of their long, heavy tails. They looked like magpies in the American West, but bigger and even clumsier. The whole country had a Great Plains feel to it, like the country around Rawlins, Wyoming, only here the antelope weren't pronghorned and all the wild ponies wore stripes. We saw the remains of a kill off the road to the right. Vultures hunched waiting in the fever trees, and marabou storks competed on the ground with jackals for the lump of red meat and torn hide that had once been a Thomson's gazelle. A tawny eagle swung down to grab a bite, but a jackal drove it off, leaping high with snapping jaws.

Then we climbed up west again out of the savannah into mountain forest, with the Aberdares looming dark and cloud-covered to the south, and suddenly it was much cooler. Blue streamers of smoke rose from the forest where men were making charcoal. Past Nyeri we swept down into the Rift Valley and onto the main road that comes south from Uganda, the A104, with its Humboldt Sink heat and potholes and the stink of unmuffled diesel exhaust from big, shabby trucks hauling coffee out of Idi Amin's nightmare world only two hundred miles to the north. Through Nakuru with the lake a tan reed-stippled sprawl off to the west, and the once-tidy Bell Hotel now flaking paint and rickety *matatus*—freelance taxis and minibuses—yapping fiercely as the morning's jackals as they darted among the heavy, bald-tired coffee lorries. The *matatus* wore names like "Kill Me Quick" and "The Professor" or "Skylab" or "Good

Friday" or "Safari to Happiness" hand painted on their sides, and they were packed tight with laughing passengers. No issue of *The East African Standard* is complete without the report of three or four fatal *matatu* crashes. You see their remains along the roadside, burnt out and crumpled. Crushed cardboard suitcases. Torn clothing, blood-blackened and not worth salvaging. Chicken feathers blowing in the wind.

*Shauri ya Mungu*, the Africans say. It is the Will of God.

We turn west on the B3, past the Longonot Satellite Station with its skeletal antennas and radar dishes etched against empty grassland, and now the Suswa Plain unrolls ahead of us, undulating waves of grassy hills reaching north to the Mau Escarpment and south to the Tanzanian border. We begin to see plains game, small herds browsing and grazing in clots on the slopes. Thomson's and Grant's gazelles, Burchell's zebras, a few giraffes stalking like stiltwalkers. At the edge of a treeline far to the right stands a conclave of eland, white daubs against the dark green of thorn at this distance.

The tarmac ends at Narok. An old-timer named Ole Pussy had a bar, restaurant, and small hotel here once, but now it is closed and we drink warm beer from the lunch box. The *dukas*—shops—are shabby, buzzing with flies, their shelves almost empty. Radios blare American rock. The last outpost of civilization. Masai elders in red *shukas* and sandals cut from truck tires stare at us from the shade of roadside stands. Long-faced, unsmiling, their spears catching the hot light. To the north the sky has gone a wrought-iron black, and the air tastes brassy with the heat of impending rain.

Then westward again, on twin-rutted red dirt, through red rock hills with candelabra trees and spiky sanseveria scratching the dark sky, onto a great sprawl of tilled plain. The plowed land is as startling as a bikini in church.

"This is the new government wheat scheme," Bill says. "Managed by Americans. All of this country from here on down to the Serengeti is ideal for grain culture. Look at the thickness of the grass where the plow hasn't turned it yet. It's like your Great Plains were a century ago. But you went and shot off your buffalo, didn't you, and put it to the plow."

The soil is black where the plows have ripped it, and on some sections the pale green haze of new wheat is already showing.

Toward evening we spotted a dark mass moving across the road ahead. Cape buffalo. Bill stopped the truck and we watched. They were moving from left to right, horns flashing from the dim red cloud of dust stirred by their hooves.

Bulls and truculent cows pulled out of the cloud to challenge us, nostrils flaring, heads up, bright black eyes fixed on the alien shape of the Land Cruiser. The dying light caught on the coruscated bosses of their horns.

"There must be a thousand of them," Bill whispered. "Look at the lovely sods move! Like a great bloody black river in spate. Don't you love it, Bwana? It was one of their kind that did my leg for me, when I got plugged, but I love them all the same. Crikey, just look at them!"

Then the light failed and the rain hit, sheeting down from the north with a thrumming roar. The road turned to grease under our wheels, and the Toyota began a four-wheel disco twitch that quickly became the theme song of this safari.

"Slip-slidin' away...."

IN THE TENT THAT NIGHT AFTER SUPPER, Bill told me how he'd been shot. I'd been home in the States when it happened, a year or so after our last safari, and hadn't heard from him in quite awhile. Then I got a short note from Bill's wife, Barbie, saying Bill had been wounded on safari and was still in the hospital. A stiff-upper-lip kind of letter that lulled me into thinking it wasn't that bad a gunshot wound. But when I arrived this time and saw how Bill was limping, how wasted the leg looked, I knew it could scarcely have been worse. He wouldn't pound the hills much anymore, forty miles a day on a bottle of water and that tough Limey grin. Not that he'd really have to.

The shooting safari business in Kenya was finished, *kufa*-ed—killed—by the sudden, nonsensical hunting ban declared by Jomo Kenyatta's government in 1976. Rumors had it that the ban was instigated by corrupt government officials who wanted to keep white hunters and their clients out of the bush so that poachers could slaughter elephants, rhinos, and other valuable game without any pesky non-African interference. On this safari Bill and I wanted to see how far that slaughter had progressed. There'd be no hunting this time, not even for birds, and Bill's guns were locked up in a vault somewhere in Nairobi. But we could still talk about hunting, and that sort of talk, for all its occasional grimness, or perhaps because of it, is the best in the world.

"It was at the Whistling Rocks, as I told you," Bill said. Outside the rain still pounded down. Moths fluttered crazily around the Coleman lamp and drowned themselves, fluttering ever more weakly, in the Scotch I'd poured for us as he talked. "I had a hunting concession in that whole stretch of country we passed through today, two thousand square miles of it. Masai country, not yet heavily hammered by the poachers. No farms in there to speak of either. The Green Hills of Africa, just about the way Hemingway saw them half a century ago. The *wainanchi*—the people thereabouts—were very friendly and helpful. We gave them plenty to eat.

"My client was an Englishwoman living on the Continent at the time. I'd hunted with her before and she was all right, a steady shot, not afraid of anything. On this particular day we were going for buffalo. How many times have I told you it's buffalo that will do you every time?" He sipped his Scotch carefully. He's not a drinking man. "It was the usual story. She wounded the buff, a nice bull, about like that first one of yours up at Tinga, and he went into cover. The old, old story. I wanted her to go back to the truck, it was too thick in there and it's less worrisome that way. But she'd have none of it.

"'Look, Ducks,' I told her, 'if you come along I'll have two things to worry about instead of just the buff.' But there were tears in her eyes." He smiled and shook his head sadly. "Okay, she got to me. I told her to stay directly behind me, though, so I'd know where she was if he charged. That was my second mistake.

"We went in, the trackers ahead and to the sides, and sure enough he was in there, waiting, hiding behind a scrap of brush you wouldn't think could hide a housecat. And he came for us, as they will. From twenty yards away.

"I could have jumped aside. I've done it many a time before. But she was there, right behind me, obedient to my orders, and the buff would have smashed her flat. I shot when he was only about five yards out and took him up the snout. Best shot of my life. He was dead when he hit me, knocked me down and groggy, for a moment at least. He was lying dead across my legs, and I could feel that the one leg was broken, pinned under his bloody great scabrous neck.

"Then I looked up and she was standing over us, with the .375 raised, pointing it at him. Her eyes were wide and out of focus. She was in shock at the suddenness of it, the horror. I started to tell her not to shoot, he was dead, I may even have actually said it. But she was beyond hearing. She shot. The bullet went through his neck and took me, just here, above the ankle."

He swatted lightly, almost blithely, at the damaged leg and moths fluttered up from the darkness.

Three hundred grains of lead and copper and nickel alloy, smashing through buffalo hair, mud, hide, bone, its jacket peeling back like a banana skin with the bullet breaking up as it tore on, spinning and keyholing, ripping out of the dead bull's neck and smashing its load of power and filth smack into his leg....

"After that it's all pretty fragmentary," Bill said. "Including my bloody foot! I remember the boys gathering around, crying. They thought I'd had it. All of them had scattered at the charge—I can't blame them—all except Lambat. He stood there as the 'bogo came, ready to shoot with the backup rifle. The client was beside herself, of course. One of the lads went back to bring up the truck. I didn't feel anything much at first, just numb for about twenty minutes or so, but I could see it was pretty bad. The whole foot was just dangling there from a few bloody shreds. I could hear the wind singing through the Whistling Rocks. Then the pain hit and I didn't think much anymore. It really felt like I was going right then. They had a tourniquet on but I felt myself going. Like we were slip-slidin' away earlier today." He hummed a few bars of the Simon and Garfunkel tune.

"They got me into the back of the truck and we headed out. I remember that as we passed a little *manyatta* thereabouts I made them stop. The day before I'd stopped to buy some eggs from a Mama I knew there and found I'd forgotten my wallet. Today I'd brought the money and I made the boys go in and pay her. I'd gotten it in my mind that I didn't want to die still owing her for those blasted *mayai*.

"We were heading for a little landing strip nearby. Someone had radioed Nairobi for a Flying Doctors plane to meet us there. I kept slipping in and out. If the plane wasn't there when we arrived at the strip, I knew I was finished. We got there. The plane hadn't. I was done for, I thought. Then the plane came.

"It was one of those little single-engined Cessnas, all they had available that day, I guess. There was the pilot and a nurse. They put me on a stretcher and into the cabin, but it was a tight squeeze and the nurse had to stand straddled over me all the way to Nairobi. I was looking up her skirt into her crotch. She had rosebuds on her knickers, I remember that. When I commented on them, she looked down at me and smiled. 'You'll be all right,' she said."

The rain had let up now, and in the silence we could hear the Mara River rushing past, nearly filling its banks. Away off in the distance I thought I could hear a lion coughing and grumbling, that far-carrying sound called *ngruma* in Swahili. But maybe it was only the night wind, or another river.

"Later, in the hospital, Lambat came to see me. I was very weak, been off my head for days, weeks maybe. The doctor had wanted to take the foot off but I made him leave it. Not that it's much good to me. I've had twenty-one operations on the bugger in the three years since it happened, and they've bloody near filleted the poor old thing."

He pulled off his specially made Wellington boot. Peeled off the sock. It looked like a baby's foot, or perhaps an albino chimpanzee's.

"That leg's now two inches shorter than the other," he said. "It's said that a man shrinks with age, but this is a hell of a way to do it."

He grinned.

"Lambat said he and the lads figured I'd be a nicer man to them from now on. The bullet must have drained all the *kali* blood out of me—all that sharp, fierce, strict blood that made me yell at them all the time. Some of them had donated blood of their own to replace mine, His Lordship among them, and with all that new, kindly, quiet, humanitarian African *damu* flowing in my veins, I could now be expected to behave in a more civilized manner. Before he left, Lambat gave me a little memento of the accident. He had it wrapped up in a handkerchief. It was a hunk of bone blown out of my leg. He'd gone back later and found it and polished it up quite nicely. I have it at home, somewhere. Must show it to you sometime."

In the morning the rain had stopped. We drove out of camp for a game run. On a ridge not far from the river, a large herd of buffalo stood against the dawn sky. When Bill drove up to them and shut off the motor, we could hear a strange thumping sound like that of a strong man slugging a tree with a wooden maul. Then the herd parted and we saw two bulls fighting at the edge of a thorn thicket. Snorting and grunting, their neck muscles bulging in the red light, they strained at one another with a combined two tons of rage. Their hooves had torn up the rich, black soil for yards around—torn it like plows in the slip-slidin' African mud. The younger of the two had broken off the tip of his right horn and his blood spurted straight up with the beating of his heart. It mingled with blood from a wound on the older bull's neck and washed down into the torn grass.

In that strange light the scene was too strong, primordial: a frame from the dawn of time. Or perhaps from its twilight.

"By God," Bill said, "don't you love the great brutes?"

# Lions & Lizards

**A** SLIVER OF MOON HUNG LOW in the African night. Beyond the flare of our campfire, lions prowled among the doum palms, drawn by the smell of the tethered camels. Now and then one of them roared—so loud and close and awful that the hair on my forearms rose and I nearly spilled my sundowner.

Delgado, though, was cool as the desert moon, smiling sardonically whenever I flinched.

We were playing a game of literary one-upmanship, taking turns with remembered quotations from prose or poetry that dealt with lions. The other fellow had to cite the source or, failing that, pay his opponent a drink. I was drinking Scotch.

Delgado was drinking beer, with now and then a puff from a hubble-bubble. Yeah, the old *bangi*.

He was the professional hunter on this safari, and a well-read one at that.

"Here's one for you," Delgado said, smirking through the flickering firelight. "'They say the Lion and the Lizard keep the Courts where Jamshyd gloried and drank deep: And Bahram, that great Hunter—the Wild Ass stamps o'er his Head, but cannot break his sleep.'"

"Easy," I said. "*The Rubaiyat of Omar Khayyam.* Fitzgerald's translation. Any moonstruck schoolboy would know it. Okay, coming back at you —'A living dog is better than a dead lion. For the living know that they shall die: but the dead know not anything.'"

"Piece of cake, *Effendi*," Delgado said, grinning winsomely through his ragged beard. Tendrils of pot-smoke wisped from his flaring nostrils. "Ecclesiastes, Chapter 9, Verses 4 and 5 of the King James Version. Any psalm-struck choirboy would know it."

He laughed, and the laugh turned into a lion's roar.

I nearly grabbed for my rifle.

Nicholas Delgado was the most unlikely white hunter in Africa. Granted, I'd met him in the Zamani region of southern Somalia, the most unlikely country I'd ever hunted, but it was more than that. First off, he was way too short—barely five feet tall in his buffalo-hide flip-flops, with shoulders so wide they looked grotesque. His hide, burned tough as biltong by the sun of the Shag, was scarred evenly on both cheeks, as if by tribal rite, or perhaps a very neat lion. He was so flat from chest to back that you felt if you folded him just right, you could fit him through the slot of a mailbox. In the second place, he scorned the starched khakis, short haircut, and ramrod-straight bearing of most professional hunters. His ratty black hair hung down to his shoulders; he usually dressed in sun-faded, cut-off Levi's and an aloha shirt.

Nick Delgado didn't stride through the wilderness—he strolled, slouched, or skulked, sometimes all three in the same languid step.

And of course he blew gage, where most PH's preferred only the most expensive single-malt Scotch—provided the client was pouring. Yet he had a reputation, from Mogadishu to the Horn of Africa, as the best lion hunter on that long, fierce, shark-haunted coast.

I'd first heard of him through "trustworthy friends" in Kenya—tales of huge black-maned desert lions winkled out of the thorn-scrub of the Upper Juba River country by a "somewhat eccentric young American, not everyone's idea of the Great White Hunter but with a marvelous instinct for *simbas*."

Like... how eccentric?

"Well, he dresses rather oddly, doesn't bathe much, and is married to not one but three of the loveliest Somali bints you've ever seen—did I mention that he's a convert to Islam? Some say his paternal grandfather occupied a high post in Italian Somaliland back in the 1920s, don't you know, and that's what drew him to the country some forty years later."

Others said he was just a wandering hippie of the '60s.

A few maintained he was a CIA plant—an agent-in-place during the chaotic days after Somalia's first president, Abdi Shermarke, was assassinated in the army coup that put Somalia in Moscow's pocket.

Whatever the truth of the matter—and Nicky Delgado would merely smile dreamy-eyed while nodding agreement to every rumor—he was a chap with a built-in lion detector. No one who had ever hunted with him had come away with less than a full-maned *simba* pegging out at ten-feet plus.

I wired Delgado at once, care of the Croce del Sud Hotel in Mog, laid on a two-week lion safari by camel into the Shag, and now here I was, camped out in the bleakest, bitterest, harshest, most thorn- and flea-bitten hunk of real estate I'd ever imagined, with a weird PH spouting poetry, a warm whiskey in my paw, a supper of greasy, half-cooked mutton turning back-flips in my belly, camels snoring and farting all around us, and the whole black Somali night, by the sound of things, full of roaringly ravenous lions. I loved every bit of it. Delgado was dead to the world, wrapped in a smelly, striped camel blanket beside the popping thorn-wood fire, no doubt dreaming the follies of The Faithful—all houris and sherbet and cool running water. I finished the last of my Dewar's, gathered up my rifle and *bilau* (the razor-sharp dagger favored by Somalis for close work), and sloped off to my own dreamland fraught with twenty-foot tall kitty-cats in fright wigs, all drooling for blood.

Dawn broke over the *Gan Libab* (Lion's Paw), a craggy, cedar-crowned rimrock bluff to our east. We'd been up for nearly two hours, breakfasted on bitter black tea and cold mutton while shivering in the shank of the desert night, then at the first hint of dawn had hiked south and east of camp under the rimrock to intercept one or more of the feeding lions who had serenaded us the previous evening as they moved off their kills to lay up till dusk

"They'll head for the cedars as soon as they've had some water," Delgado explained. "It's cool up there in the heat of the day. Then tonight, they'll either return to the kill or possibly hunt again."

At about the time when we could first distinguish a white thread from a black, Delgado's chief tracker—a skinny, biltong-tough Somali from the Haud called Omar Karim—raised his hand in the universal sign for "Halt!" Ahead of us in the darkness I could see a darker thing moving. But it was too tall, too elongate for a lion. A man emerged from the gloom, then two more. Their spears stood spiky as sisal stalks against the reddening sky. Delgado knelt and covered them with his rifle—an ugly, battered, short-barreled .505 Gibbs with a hog-ivory front sight that winked like a star—while Karim went forward to palaver. He shouted something back to us in Arabic.

"It's okay," Delgado said. "They're herdsmen. This country is full of *shifta*—bandits who'd kill you for the threads on your back, then cut off your balls for earrings. You can never be too careful in the Shag. But these guys are harmless." We could hear sheep bleating now, and I noticed a few scrawny, acrobatic goats playing Nadia Comaneci on the outlying scree of the rimrock. We walked down to join the conclave.

"These dudes say a big brute of a lion got in among their herd last night," Delgado translated. "Smote 'em hip and thigh—killed about a dozen head. Would have been more except the kid who was watching the herd went after the *simba* with his spear. He put it in him, more than once, but then the lion swatted him—finished him right there with one punch." One of the herdsmen stepped forward, a dark, proud man with that hawk-like nose and fuzzy-wuzzy hairdo of the Shag, and showed us the boy's spear, or what was left of it. The soft iron had been twisted like a corkscrew by the lion's gyrations, then bent in an open-mouthed U. Coarse, yellow hair clung to the lacquer-like blood that was drying on the cockeyed blade and shaft. The spearhead smelled of smoke and raw meat.

"Where's the herdboy?"

"The lion went off with him," Delgado said. "He's eating him right now, up there in the cedars."

The morning's mutton performed a cartwheel on the balance beam of my gut. Then two or three more in rapid succession. Olympic judges would have given the performance at least a nine-point-three.

"What do you say, Effendi?" Delgado was grinning at me, eyes sparkling like topaz in the blood-red dawn. A change had come over him, or so it seemed in that eerie light. Gone was the spaced-out, laid-back, hippy-dippy scuzzball of the previous evening, and before me stood a hunter, taut and twanging and eager for the chase. His scruffy beard seemed to have filled out, thickened magically somehow, along with his hair, into a lion's mane. He quivered like a gundog on point. "Let's get that dude while he's still feeding."

"Right on, bro," I said. Delgado gave me a funny look, as if I'd done something inappropriate in an art gallery—like dropped my pants.

At that moment the sun burst clear of the rimrock and the whole world changed. It was as if someone had opened the gates of hell. The heat of the day pounded us like a left hook courtesy of Smokin' Joe Frazier, the light level jumped and pegged at six-kajillion lumens, driving bright steel needles into my eyeballs. The Shag lay revealed in all its awful splendor—a sprawl of rock and sand carpeted in aloe and sansevieria, grown thick with gray, brittle thorn scrub that clawed at your face like frenzied cats at every step. A mottled, dirty red scorpion as long as André the Giant's middle finger scuttled across my desert boot, paused to wave hello with his front pincers, then dove into the sand like Greg Louganis, without a ripple. I shuddered and looked around for more.

"Cool breeze it, man," Delgado said, watching me. "Scorpions come with the territory—make you sick as hell, but they can't kill you, much less eat you." He chuckled in his beard. "Now sand vipers are something else again. Particularly the Egyptian sawscaled variety. Hemotoxic as hell—blow your leg up like the Goodyear blimp in about five seconds. They're easily riled, so try not to step on one."

The Somali herdsmen had led us to the scene of the slaughter. The bodies of sheep lay all over the landscape, some with crushed skulls, others lying bent and crooked with broken necks or backs. A few of the cripples still struggled weakly.

A Somali woman looked up from where she was skinning out one of the cripples (nothing goes to waste in the Shag). She almost took my breath away with her huge dark eyes under finely sculpted brows, a long, hawk-like nose reminiscent of Cher's, wide, sultry, delicately curved lips, and skin the texture and color of café espresso into which a few drops of heavy cream had been stirred. One of the herdsmen caught me looking at her and put his hand on his *bilau*. He barked a few words in Somali and she disappeared into the thorn-scrub. The half-skinned but still living sheep she'd been working on bleated once or twice, as if begging her to stay.

"This is where the boy stuck the lion," Delgado said. There was remarkably little blood—a few sprays of bright blood already crystallizing on the sand in stringy patterns, and a large, dark clot roughly the shape of Africa, with smaller dark clots trailing off like islands in the direction of the rimrock. "He put it in his gut," Delgado said. "More's the pity." He stood and looked up toward the ridge, dark-topped with its thick, dwarfed cedars. "He's gonna be one mighty sore pussycat when we come up on him. All right, let's be havin' him."

The spooring was easy—a good blood trail every few yards and soft sand in which the lion's nine-inch pugmarks stood out like road signs allowed us to track him well wide of his trail. Karim stayed closest to the track, about five yards to the left of it. Delgado was ten yards to the right and I followed behind him, another five yards to starboard.

Already the sand was broiling hot. I sunk in over the tops of my *veld-schoon* with every step, filling them with gritty fire, and began to see the wisdom of Delgado's flip-flops. They spilled the burning sand out after each stride. Sweat was no problem: The aridity of the Shag sucked the moisture off your brow as soon as it popped to the surface. After a few hundred yards, though, I began to feel a raw, itchy chafing in my crotch and armpits. My shorts and bush shirt were crusted in salt from evaporated sweat. Delgado had shed his cutoffs back at the site of the sheep kill and was wearing only his long, loose, cotton aloha shirt, which came down to midthigh and thus protected his groin from thorns and other nasties. The sun-faded aloha shirt—originally green, black, and gold in pat-

tern—also served as a kind of camouflage, I saw. As we entered the dark
dwarf cedars, it broke up his silhouette admirably. He'd tied his long hair
back with a thong of camel hide to keep it out of his eyes and the shrubbery as well. There was method in his madness, sure enough.

On the edge of the cedars he stopped and motioned me over to him.
Karim had stopped, too, and was squatting on his heels, Delgado's back-up
weapon in his hands—a heavy, thorn-scarred, ten-bore Boss loaded with
SSG which, from the state of the blueing on its gaping twin tubes, had
been knocking around Africa since the early Eocene. But again it was a
good choice. No less an authority than Dennis Lyell's friend, an old Africa
hand named Norman Smith who had killed hundreds of *simbas*, said in a
1916 letter to Lyell, "If I knew I was in for a lion charge I would rather
have a shotgun with big shot, AAA, or SSG, than any rifle, and should not
fire my first barrel until he was within 20 feet. I don't think he would
reach me."

I eased over to Delgado, walking on the sides of my feet to minimize
the snapping of rotten thorn twigs underfoot. "He's just ahead in there,"
Delgado whispered. "Hear him?"

At first all I could hear was the pulse beating in my ears like a fast surf
on a lion-stalked beach. Then I heard it—the ugly, meaty crunch of feline
back teeth slicing through flesh and bone, followed by a soft grunt, then
the sound of a huge, sandpaper tongue lapping viscous liquid. "He went
into this thick stuff right here," Delgado breathed, toeing a pugmark with
his flip-flop. "*Ex unque leonem.* 'From his claw you can tell a lion'—but
you can't tell him much." He grinned at me, the scars on his cheeks wrinkling under the bristly whiskers. "We're going to circle out to the left a
ways, get the breeze dead in our faces, then move in until we see him.
And at that point, Effendi, it's up to you."

"Isn't it awfully thick in there?" My whisper came out as dry and
crunchy as the searing sandstone underfoot. "How close can we actually
get to him?"

What I really meant was, "How far can we stay away?"

"Maybe ten, fifteen yards if we're lucky. Right on top of him if need
be. But it's quiet going in there—cedar needles and rock. Hey, this isn't
like Kenya or Tanganyika where you pop them from 200 yards out. This is
the real thing—up close and personal. No scopes in my country. That's
why I told you to bring iron sights. If he comes, you've got about a second, second and a half to up on him and shoot." He grinned again, the
catlike, wrinkled grin that wasn't at all humorous. "Just think of it as low-
level wingshooting—a low, fast-approaching bird that's going to pass right

between your legs. If you can, get down on one knee when he comes—in this thick stuff you've got no mobility anyway. A lion's about four feet high at the shoulder. You're better off shooting at the level of his face than shooting down at him. But you know all that already. Anyway, shoot him right in the kisser—right into that big black hole rimmed with teeth. I'll be backing you with the Gibbs, and Karim's got the stopper—the ten-bore. You up for it?"

"I guess so."

"Take a hit of water," he said handing me his felt-covered canteen.

I washed the bitterness out of my mouth with a long swig of warm *aqua*-not-so-*pura*, swallowed it, and handed the canteen back to Delgado. He hung the strap over his shoulder and neck, with the canteen dangling down his back. A strange, not-unpleasant aftertaste lingered on my taste buds.

"Okay," I said, suddenly confident, "let's rock 'n' roll. Let's macerate that maneater. Let's levitate that lousy lion into the hyperion. I'm plumb froze for cat meat, podner."

I never found out what he'd spiked the water with—Electric Kool-Aid *a la* Ken Kesey?—but whatever it was, it did the job.

"'There was a swarm of bees and honey in the carcass of the lion,'" Delgado said, smiling mysteriously. "Book of Judges, I don't remember the chapter and verse."

"'Out of the eater came forth meat,'" I countered, grinning back at him. "'And out of the strong came forth sweetness.' Ditto."

We headed into the cedars, smiling, with death in our hearts.

THEY SAY MEN TAKE ON THE CHARACTERISTICS of the animals they kill in fair chase. Certainly it was true of Delgado. He moved through the cedar thickets as silently as a stalking lion, crawling on his belly where need be, flat as a lion against the quiet rocks, boneless and supple as a lion while he weaved through the boulders. The rock was red where it wasn't black in shadow, a dancing webwork of dark and light. Karim was out on the left flank, moving as quietly as a shadow himself. His eyes were squinted slits, his lips locked tight—the African stalker's insurance against a giveaway gleam of teeth or eye-whites that might inadvertently alert the prey. I followed as best I could, a few feet to Delgado's right. Maybe it was the intense concentration of the stalk, maybe the weird drink from Delgado's canteen, but I don't believe I've ever moved more silently or with more confidence in half a century of hunting than I did on that hot, breathless morning in the Shag.

Everything was heightened, screwed down to the breaking point. The buzz of a camel fly ten yards away sounded like a low-level strafing run from a squadron of Warthog antitank jets. The plangent scream of a hawk-eagle high in the Somali sun was distinguishable note for note. The smell of cedar gum, oozing from scarred bark, filled the day with acrid sweet perfume. Then I smelled blood—rich, rusty, sweeter than cedar—and the sharp, hot stink of leaking guts. The lion and his victim—or what was left of the poor kid—lay straight ahead. But I could not see them. Delgado stopped, crouching with his hand behind him, palm toward me.

I stopped.

Karim stopped.

Time stopped.

I could hear the lion lapping blood. About five feet ahead of us. A steady lap, lap, lap, intermixed with the heavy, rasping sound of his purr—a cement mixer running rough. I could smell that thick, hot, sour smell of the cat house now, too—memories of boyhood visits to the Milwaukee Zoo where the big, grave lions looked up slowly behind steel bars and riveted me with their cool amber eyes. I loved them then, their slouching arrogance, their regal hauteur. I loved them and wanted to touch them. But even then I knew I would have to kill them first to perform such an act of *lèse majesté*. What does Shakespeare say in *As You Like It*? "The hind that would be mated by the lion must die for love." No thanks. I loved this lion now, but he would have to die for *my* love....

A sudden, violent gust of the hot *kharif* wind set the scene in motion. It lifted the cedar boughs and set them tossing madly. It unmasked the man-eater and I saw him for the first time—black-maned, huge, his massive head blocky as an anvil wreathed in black lightning, red-jowled, dripping blood and bile on the cracked white ribs and torn pink fluff of the herdboy's lungs, one of the boy's arms hung out limply toward us as if in supplication. The lion lay propped on his elbows, one giant paw pinning the body at the neck, angled three quarters toward us, his haunches gathered under him like coiled springs, flies buzzing ecstatically over the boy's empty body cavity and the dark, ugly stab wound in the lion's side—and the lion, the lion of my dreams and all our nightmares, looked at us....

Looked straight into my eyes, not ten yards away.

"Now!" Delgado yelled. "Whack him!"

The rifle floated to my shoulder—the Remington Model 700 BDL in .375 H&H ("Use Enough Gun," the man said)—as the lion sprang straight toward us. One bound, I'm sure of it, and then he was airborne. All hair and teeth and claws, wrapped in an ugly grating, grunting snarl that seemed to fill the universe, so loud that I never heard the shot with which I killed him....

Impressions: Delgado rolling catlike to the left and mounting the Gibbs to his shoulder even as he rolled to his knees as the lion passed overhead; Karim on one knee to the side with the Boss glaring black-muzzled, tracking the ballistic arc of the flying lion; the lion hanging huge above me as I crouched and swung with him and shot—seeing the ribs cave in to the two-ton punch of the 300-grain Silvertip; another grunt as it hit and knocked him off course....

Then I too was rolling sideways. Out from under. A dead lion can still have a lot of life in him—a 500-pound Cuisinart with poisonous blades, being pulsed by a spastic madman, would do less harm if you chanced to fall into it. The Gibbs spoke just once —ker-whang—as I worked my bolt. Delgado paying the insurance. Finished.

Nick walked over and prodded the lion's staring eye with his rifle muzzle. No blink. He grinned over at me and reached into his aloha shirt for matches and a Bangi Bomber. "Do you know Donne's 'Farewell to Love'? There's a nice riff in there, goes, 'Ah cannot we, as well as cocks and lions jocund be after such pleasures?'" He laughed and fired up another smoke.

We finished out the safari on plains game—beisa oryx, dibatag, gerenuk, and beira. The Shag is generous to its children if they can take the heat and know where to look. I grew to love the Somalis, those arrogant, thieving, murderous, brave, generous, admirably able survivors in a world full of man-eaters—not just the lions that follow their herds for a living, but the Shag itself, which eats strong men for breakfast.

Nicky Delgado was a strong man, but in the end it devoured him, too. He was caught up, finally, in the insane warfare with Ethiopia in 1977 on the Ogaden Plateau that destroyed Somalia's leftist army and wiped out Soviet influence as well. Perhaps the CIA rumor wasn't nonsense. Nicky Delgado hasn't been heard from since. But I will always remember him for his steady, tough grace under pressure, his instant transformation once the game was afoot from hippie to hunter.

Perhaps the most fitting epitaph for him comes from the Psalms: "The young lions roar after their prey, and seek their meat from God."

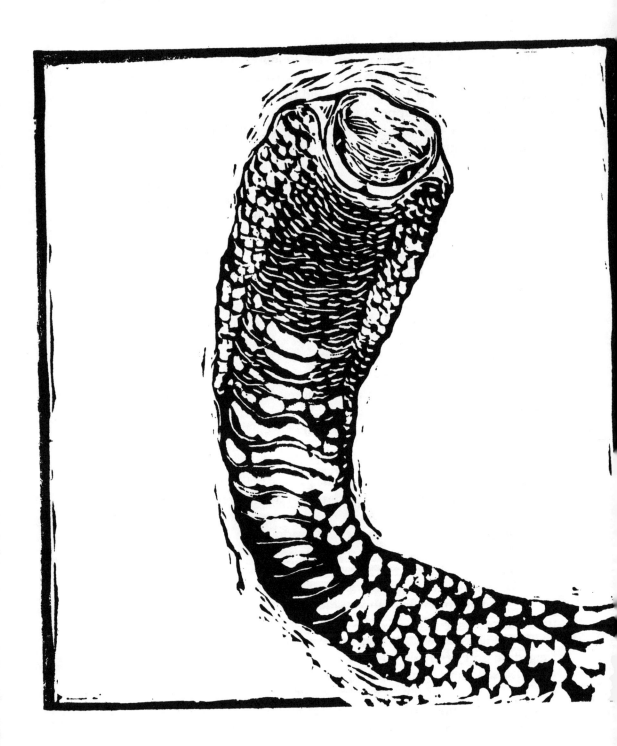

# Never on Sunday

IN SIX SAFARIS THROUGH THE WILDEST PARTS of East Africa, I've seen only three snakes in the bush. One was a small sand boa, basking peacefully on the rocks at Lake Rudolph one day while I was fly-casting for tigerfish. Another, which lived in the thatched roof of a *banda* I stayed in down on the Coast, was a brown house snake, a non-toxic constrictor that eats a lot of mice and insects. Though it is prone to nip a lot when first captured, it's said to make a pleasant and beneficial household pet once it's been tamed.

The third was a very long, thick snake we found in a hole along the Ewaso Nyiro River one morning. Its head was sticking out of one end of the hole—an abandoned warthog burrow—and its tail out the other end. The holes were about ten feet apart. Lambat saw it first and warned us to get back. He said later that it had spread its hood, so it was clearly some kind of cobra. Later we described the snake to Peter Bramwell, our snake-catcher friend from the Coast.

"Was the color a dull black or was it rather a sort of dirty-pewter hue?" he asked.

Dull black, we said.

"Was its head short, about as wide as it was deep, and a bit distinct from its neck? Or was the head square and rather bulldoggish about the snout?"

What you said first, we said.

"Were its eyes about medium-sized, or were they great huge ones that you noticed right off—as it were, a woodcock's eye as distinct from a pheasant's?"

Nothing special, we said.

"Then it was a black-necked cobra, sometimes called the spitting cobra," Peter said. "*Naja nigricollis*. Nasty chap, old *Naja*. Hunts by night and lies up by day, usually in an old termite nest or an abandoned pig hole. *Naja's* first line of defense is to shoot for the eyes. It's a neurotoxic venom, of course, as with all cobras, and strongly acidic. I've tested these chaps and they can spit nineteen to twenty-one times before running dry. At eighteen feet they'll spray you from head to toe. At twelve feet they'll hit you spang in both eyes, every time. Remarkably accurate, old *Naja*. Because they're nocturnal, you usually have no warning of their presence before it's too late. Within four seconds of a hit, you're reeling out of the way in pain. It feels like a kick in the goolies, except that the pain isn't localized in your groin—you feel it all through your body. I always carry eyedrops—adrenaline, one part in two thousand—and with that one can stop the pain in ten seconds.

"Untreated, the pain will last for five days. That is, if you happen to live that long. The poison can enter the minute blood vessels of the eye by osmosis. Unsweetened milk is the next best eyewash to the adrenaline solution. But it must be unsweetened. The sugar in sweet milk will cause the venom to stick to your eyeballs. Water is less effective than milk, though it's often the only recourse. In a real pinch, ugly as it sounds, you could ask a companion to urinate in your eyes—anything to flush out the poison. It's also a good idea, when after spitting cobras, not to shave. That's why I wear this beard. A single drop of that toxin in a shaving nick and you're for it."

Why hadn't the snake we saw spat at us, we asked. After all, we were well within range.

"He was probably playing dead," Peter said. "They'll do that, you know. Old *Naja* is not really all that aggressive. They only spit when they feel threatened. But since they're quite shy and nervous, they often do feel threatened."

Peter began catching snakes—"for the fun of it"—in 1940, when he was twelve years old, and only took to it professionally in 1964, soon after Uhuru. He reckons he's caught more than a thousand snakes over the years, selling them to zoos in Europe and to producers of antivenins worldwide. The meat of some snakes, particularly the big African rock python that can exceed twenty feet in length, is considered a delicacy in parts of Asia. And of course their beautifully marked, finely scaled skins often end up as handbags, boots, and purses. It's a pity, Peter feels. They tame quite readily and enjoy being handled. At Peter's serpentarium near Kilifi Creek on the Coast, I was once presented with a necklace of live pythons. Peter draped two pythons—together weighing one hundred thirty pounds—over my shoulders. They coiled cool and smooth around my neck, distributing their weight so evenly over my arms and shoulders that I had no trouble holding them. As one of them stared into my eyes from inches away and tasted the tip of my nose with its tongue, a small African boy stood watching with awe. "That *mzee*," he said of me, "is no coward." I felt quite proud.

In 1977, Peter was bitten by a black mamba. "Until then," he told us, "no one had ever survived the bite of a black mamba. I'd been bitten by boomslangs, puff adders, and once by a green mamba, but had pulled through all right. Yet when the black bit me, I thought for sure I'd had it. It happened on a Sunday. I should have known better than to try to capture that snake. All my bites have come on a Sunday."

Bramwell was at home that day, near Kilifi, when one of his household staff reported that a snake was lurking near the rabbit hutches. "I found it up on the rafters in the garage, and I could see at once that it was a black," he recalls. "I got my catching tongs—they're rather like the tongs grocery clerks use to take packages and cans from a high shelf, but with the gripping ends padded so as to avoid injuring the snake—and got the leather-necked catching bag ready. Then I grabbed him with the tongs. But too far back. About eighteen inches of his head and neck were forward of the grips. Nonetheless I stuffed him in the bag, but when I went to close it my hand was too near the leather mouth of the sack. The snake was still on the tongs but he got his head over the edge and hit me on the hand. Twice. I whipped him out of the bag and killed him—grabbed him by the tail and whipped his head against the concrete floor. I remember shouting, 'I've killed you, you bastard—but you're not killing me.' Pure bravado—whistling in the dark, you know.

"That was about 9:30 in the morning. There was no pain. Not like a puff adder's bite, which feels like toothache from the top of your head to the soles of your feet. That's what a hemotoxic poison will do to you. But neurotoxins, like those of the mamba family, affect the central nervous system, ultimately shutting off the victim's ability to breathe and even stopping the heartbeat. Apart from the puncture wounds, there is no appreciable pain. Quite the opposite—a pleasant ennui settles over one toward the end."

In twenty minutes, Peter was feeling "pins and needles" in his extremities. Realizing that their Toyota Land Cruiser would be too slow for the emergency run to the nearest hospital, Peter's wife Jan borrowed a neighbor's Mercedes sedan and drove Peter to Mombasa, about fifty miles away, at speeds up to eighty-five miles an hour. By the sheerest good luck, a British snakebite expert was in the hospital's operating theatre when the Bramwells arrived. "He dropped everything and came to the rescue. He pulled me through," Peter says. "Three days later I learned that a chap in

South Africa had also been bitten by a black mamba and had survived. We two were the first ever to make it. And both in the same bloody week."

But the after effects of the poison and its treatment have left Bramwell feeling limp, washed out, lethargic, without much zest for the hard physical work he once enjoyed in his days as a hunter, game warden, and police officer in the years before Uhuru.

"The effect of these poisons is cumulative," he says. "My uncle, Alan Tarlton, was a snake catcher for years. During World War II, when there was a great demand for antivenins, he never had fewer that four hundred puff adders in his cages. He was bitten forty-five times by old *Bitis arietans*—to give the puffer his full Linnean due—and he claimed that after the forty-third bite he was immune. The forty-fifth bite killed him."

I'VE OFTEN FOUND IT CURIOUS that when Americans ponder Africa's dangers, they worry more about snakes than the other, more formidable hazards of the continent. They seem to have no fear at all of the larger mammals. Perhaps television, with its Everything-Is-Beautiful approach to wildlife, is responsible for this naivete. But lions, leopards, elephants, rhinos, hippos, and buffalo still kill many people every year in Africa, and crocodiles kill even more. Not long ago in the Masai-Mara, a former white hunter I know was guiding some wealthy American women on a birdwatching safari through that northern extension of the Serengeti Plain. One evening at sundown they went out for a stroll. They were accompanied by an armed *askari*, just in case. Suddenly a bull buffalo appeared out of the weeds and attacked them, without provocation. It smashed one of the women to the ground and crushed her to death with the craggy boss of its horns. It hooked the other woman and injured her critically. When the former white hunter grabbed the bull's horn and tried to pull it away, it turned and threw him up into the fork of a thorn tree, then smashed him in the testicles. The *askari* shot the buffalo with his .303 Lee-Enfield but only wounded it. The buff finally trotted off, its anger spent. The dead woman's family sued the safari outfitters who had arranged the trip. The lawyers claimed that the dead woman did not know there were any dangerous animals left in Africa....

Perhaps the most dangerous animals in Africa, though, are the ones too small to be seen. Some of them can kill you as dead as any buffalo can, though not as swiftly or spectacularly. And even if they don't kill you, you may wish they had. These small beasts are the microorganisms and viruses that cause amoebic dysentery, bilharzia, giardiasis, hookworm, onchocerciasis (or "blinding worm"), kala-azar, leprosy, meningitis, plague, typhoid fever, typhus, yaws, cholera, cerebral malaria, *nagana* (or "sleeping sickness"), green monkey disease, and its close relative, AIDS.

As Pliny the Elder put it two thousand years ago, "*Ex Africa semper aliquid novi.*" Out of Africa, always something new.

# A Hippo Hunt

THESE WANDOROBO TODAY, they're not the real item," Peter Bramwell said. We were drinking shandy on the verandah of a lodge in Kilifi, just below Malindi on the Coast. Peter was in good voice. He was a snake-catcher now, semi-retired since that mamba bit him a couple of years ago and he nearly died, but he still ran a roadside herpetarium near the ferry landing at Kilifi Creek and did a steady business eliciting shudders from the passing tourists. In the old days, before snakes got into his blood, he hunted crocodiles for their hides down along the Rufiji River in what was then Tanganyika.

"I knew some real 'Dorobos down there," he said. "Did I ever tell you of the hippo hunt?"

"I don't believe so," Bill said. "Pray, do." He nudged my foot under the table: Hear this!

"They were wee, *wizened* little buggers, these 'Dorobos," Peter began, drawing out the "z" and wrinkling his face quite awfully. "Small and scrawny, not much bigger than pygmies, and they dressed in skins if anything at all. The *mzee* who led the band had a white beard, his hair all grizzled and hoary. I'd been shooting crocs down below and as I came up the river, I saw some *kiboko*, that's hippos, don't you know, (this for my benefit, as if Americans perforce knew no Swahili) sporting around in the water as they will near a big matted raft of papyrus that had fetched up in a back eddy. A bit farther on I came upon these 'Dorobos and told them about the hippopotami. The old man said they would kill one. Did I want some of the fat? It makes splendid cooking oil, you know. Some prefer it to rhino fat, or even lion. I thanked him, no, but said I would enjoy observing their method of taking hippo. The *mzee* said that would be jolly good.

"I led them back to where I'd seen the hippos at play, but they had disappeared. 'They're under the papyrus,' the *mzee* said. I watched from the bank as he made his preparations. He removed a crudely barbed iron spearhead from a bamboo carrying case and mounted it on a long thin shaft of reed—about twelve feet long, I'd say—then smeared it very carefully with poison from another container. They boil the poison down from the inner bark of the aconcanthera, reducing it to a thick, black, noxious-smelling glue. Often, he told me, they'll boil a shrew in it as well. Why? you ask. So that the essence of the shrew, that most persistent little murderer, will carry the poison to the animal's vitals! The spearhead was long and slim, like a snake's head, its fang-like barbs now deadly with the wicked, freshly applied poison."

Again the long "z" this time in "poison."

Peter continued.

"Where precisely were the *kiboko*? Near the upstream end of the papyrus raft, of course. If I looked closely, the *mzee* said, I could see it lifting and falling, very gently, from the breathing of the hippos. Indeed it was so. The *mzee* stripped off his monkey-skin *shuka* and walked naked out onto the reeds. They were clustered thickly, two or three feet, maybe more, and he picked his way across them in the most gingerly fashion, walking light and swift as a sandpiper, and with the same insouciance, but obviously studying the surface of the raft quite closely to ensure against breaking through. I doubt the old chap weighed more than six or seven stone—well under one hundred pounds—and he stood no taller than a schoolboy. Now and then he paused to probe the reeds with the butt of his spear. He listened, he watched, he felt with his toes."

Peter stood from the table on the veranda to mimic the old man's actions, a fearful look of wide-eyed caution on his own poison-raddled face. A few of the other customers—German tourists up from Mombasa—turned in their seats to stare at him in puzzlement.

"It was dusk now, that sudden equatorial dusk when the light turns a poisonous green and every riverside leaf seems etched on the sky in India ink. The Rufiji ran past, red as blood, and there was the old *mzee*, frail and naked as one of those stick figures you see in the caves of Altamira, killing bison and mammoth and wooly rhinoceros, and now this fragile hunter about to attack a creature that could snap him in half like this...."

Peter snapped a matchstick in his fingers. Germans jumped two tables away. Now Peter sat and leaned forward, his eyes hooded and cautious, every sense alert. For a moment, with the low sunset light leaching the color from his whiskers and goatee, he and the *mzee* were the same man, hunting.

"At last he found what he sought. He peered. He listened. He reversed the spear once more and eased the thin butt down, down through the reeds, probing slowly and ever so carefully, the spearpoint slim and black high above his bent head. Then the spear stopped. He held its shaft lightly between his palms and looked over to me, where I stood on the shore. He smiled his toothless smile. The shaft, I saw, was rising and falling, rising and falling—the bull kiboko, breathing there under the papyrus."

Peter smiled across the table at us, his eyes young with wonder.

"Then gently the old man withdrew his probe. He reversed the spear yet again, this time point down. Again he eased it down through the reeds until the point stopped. He shifted his hands up the spear shaft until they were extended at arms' length over his head. His face seemed old as time itself. Then he leapt into the air like an Olympian, locked his spindly shanks around the spear shaft, and drove it with his whole weight down through the reeds and deep into the massive body of his prey...."

Beer bottles clanked and canted ominously as Peter drove both fists, one atop the other, down onto the tabletop. Again the Germans jumped, staring around at us this time with vexed looks on their beefy faces.

"The papyrus raft heaved as if a depth bomb had exploded beneath it. The spear shaft leapt upward, then disappeared as if sucked down into the muddy depths of the river itself. The bull *kiboko* sounded, swift as a harpooned whale. The *mzee* scampered like a squirrel back over the reeds to the safety of the shore. He was grinning hugely as he ran, and as he neared me I could hear him cackling to himself—Hé, hé, hé!"

Peter paused for effect, looking dangerously at the Germans, and took a long, final swig from his shandy.

"Next morning as I walked out to hunt, I saw the 'Dorobos tugging the bloated body of the hippo ashore. The *mzee* was directing them, standing knee deep in the river, wrapped in his black and white shawl of monkey fur, chewing on a thick slab of hippo fat."

Peter nodded across the table at us. "That's how the real Wandorobo did it."

# PART
# FOUR
# NYANGAO

*An old man lies dying in a field on the outskirts of Nanyuki. At one corner of this foreign field, a garbage tip smolders behind a row of cheap shops lining the highway. The sun pounds down through a stiff southwesterly breeze, and the smoke flattens toward a hut not far away. The hut is built of flattened tins and lifeless branches whose dead leaves flap in the acrid wind. Dirty rags plug some of the holes. Inside the hut, seated on the skulls of cattle, three men and a woman are drinking tea from chipped enamel mugs. A small fire crackles. Outside in the sun lies what looks like a bundle of twigs wrapped in a faded red blanket. But something stirs for a moment, black skin through the rips in the wrapping. It's old Nyangao, the Hyena, the Eater of Meat, and he is the man who is dying.*

"Finished," Bill says. "The poor old sod doesn't even know we're here. When I first met him twenty-odd years ago, he was a big, strong chap with bracelets above his biceps and wrist-knives on his arms. His head was plastered in blue clay interwoven with ostrich plumes and the hair of his ancestors. The old time Turkana never got a haircut until they died. Then their sons cut it off and wove it into their own hairpieces. Great shaggy periwigs, they were." Bill shakes his head sadly as he looks at his old friend. "He told me he was full grown before he ever saw a white man. He must be close to a hundred years old by now. But look at him. He's got an appointment with the Big Barber in the Sky any day now."

*The woman on the cattle skull says she is Nyangao's granddaughter. We give her twenty-five shillings—about three dollars—to buy milk and tobacco. Maybe it will ease the old man's passing. More likely, though, it will buy beer and* murungi *for the hut's healthier occupants. Murungi is the bitter, leafy upper twigs of a tree that grows in the East African uplands. The Arabs call it* khat, *and it's been written up in* High Times. *Murungi produces a mildly elevating effect, not unlike a weak amphetamine, and African* askaris *and hunters chew it regularly to keep them alert and immune to cold or pain through their long watches. Right now the old Eater of Meat could use about a bale of the stuff.*

*At the sound of our voices the old man wakes up. He stares up blankly through crusted eyelids and finally recognizes Bill. He offers his hand to each of us in turn. It feels fragile, that hand, a fistful of a dry tinder wrapped in grease paper.*

"Habari yako, Rafiki?" *Bill says. What news, Friend.*

"Mzuri sana," *the old man replies. Very good indeed.*

He and Bill talk about old times, heartily cursing the modern ones, and Bill pointedly informs Nyangao of the money we'd given his granddaughter. In fact, he gives the old man another twenty-five shillings just to make sure. The granddaughter averts her eyes as the old man glares at her. He will get his milk and tumbaco. Maybe even a quid of murungi.

As we drive away, Bill shakes his head again.

"It's all finished, Bwana. Not just that old man there. In a few years it will all be gone. The old way, the warriors, perhaps even the game. That dying old Turkana is just one more manifestation of it. When he was young, he told me, he marched clear across the Suguta Desert drinking nothing but the sweat he could scrape from his armpits. Imagine it! In those days they raided cattle from the neighboring tribes—Rendile and Suk and Samburu—and they killed their enemies in the most horrible manner imaginable. And laughed when they were captured and tortured in turn. Now he's dying in a field behind a garbage tip. It's all wrong, Bwana. He should be dying up north in his homeland by Basso Narok—Lake Rudolph, surrounded by weeping grandchildren. They'd be trying to force-feed him on crocodile stew and fried ants. Offering him calabashes of that bitter, greasy lake water. The wind would be howling down off the Kulal, that big flat-topped mountain east of the lake, all sand and salty foam, and the doum palms creaking, great green bitter waves crashing along the western shore. Ah yes, then he could peg with honour!"

Kirinyaga rose ahead of us, what we whites call Mount Kenya, blue and white in the afternoon sun. At the Safari Club a while later, ice chinked cooly in cocktail glasses and the smell of perfume drifted downwind from the girls laughing and plucking at their bikinis beside the pool. Down below us, Nanyuki and the old man's hut were lost in the haze.

# Farewell to Africa

BRAIN-SHOT, THE FIRST TWO ELEPHANTS had dropped in their tracks. They lay side by side in the trampled thorn scrub like huge, deflated hot-air balloons. The third elephant, a young bull, had taken a bullet through the left shoulder. He'd managed to run about a hundred yards farther than his sisters, spewing bright lung blood from his trunk all the way. Then he collapsed on his right side and died.

The *shifta*—perhaps as many as five of them, judging by the tracks they'd left—had hacked out the tusks with axes and *pangas*, then cut brush to cover the bodies. That would keep vultures off and delay discovery of the slaughter by anti-poaching units and their aerial reconnaissance patrols until the *shifta* had moved on. But now, two weeks later, the vultures had arrived, along with the marabou storks. They circled on thermals, high overhead, or squatted, waiting, on the few sparsely leafed trees surrounding the kills. The early arrivals had scrabbled through the brush covering the carcasses and begun to feed. The obscene icing of their droppings left strange, unreadable runes of whitewash on the wrinkled, deliquescent hides of the dead elephants.

They hadn't been big elephants, far from it. Teenagers or young adults at best. Not very much ivory. The young bull had carried perhaps eight or ten pounds to the tusk, the others no more than five.

Forty pounds of ivory, all together, more or less.

At $120 a pound on the world market, as it was then, that would come to $4,800, of which the poachers—for the price of three bullets—would realize 25 percent, or $1,200.

If they divided the profits five ways, that would be $240 a man.

For 6,000 Kenya shillings, say $300, a would-be poacher or bandit can "rent" a Heckler & Koch G-3 rifle and six rounds of 7.62mm ammunition, if he knows the right sources (usually the police).

These poachers,though,had brought their own tools from Somalia, where guns and ammo are almost as abundant as camels after more than two decades of non-stop warfare. Annual per capita income in Kenya is $290,in Somalia $228. Not a bad investment,if you don't mind walking a long way through hot,arid thorn scrub to place your shots.

The blood thrown from the young bull's trunk had dried on the red, hard-baked laterite soil in loose,eerie,almost graceful patterns.

The effect was that of an action painting,a gigantic,unframed Jackson Pollock,black lacquer on a red ground. But already the *chungu*—soldier ants—were busily deconstructing it. Long chains of them mutated from the killing ground,each chain seemingly endless,each ant bearing away a big flake of dried blood. The soles of the elephant's feet had peeled away in death and they now lay like the hunks of blown truck tires that you see along the Interstates.

The ants would get to them eventually.

Nothing goes to waste in Africa,except life.

The sun was hot,the stench of death everywhere: thick,sweet,acrid, rotten,filling the dead air so that even mouth-breathing didn't help. You could still taste it. And the taste of death is worse than the smell. The only sound was the buzzing of the flies.

I'D COME AGAIN TO EAST AFRICA to assess the state of the wildlife and see what hope,if any,remained for it in the future. The safari began,fittingly enough,in January of 1990—the first month of the last decade of the 20th Century—and a *fin de siècle* mood pervaded the entire six weeks of our safari. I'd traveled sub-Saharan Africa many times before. My first visit was in 1964,in the first flush of black African inde- pendence,and on this trip I hoped to see how the continent's Pleistocene heritage had fared under a quarter of a century's stewardship by post- colonial governments. In five trips since that initial safari,I'd seen wildlife dwindle drastically—slowly at first,then with increasing momentum as human populations growing at more than three percent a year had filled formerly wild lands with cattle,sheep,goats,tin-roofed villages,and inex- orably spreading cultivation. Areas where I'd once seen herds of antelope and zebra,elephants and rhino,feeding undisturbed except by natural predators and the occasional hunting safari (which takes only one or two animals out of one hundred—old males near the end of their breeding years—and pays handsomely at that for the privilege),were now covered in wheat schemes, onion farms, and cattle. The human population of Kenya, the country I knew best, had nearly trebled, from about ten million in 1964 to some twenty-five million at the beginning of 1990. That number will double again in seventeen years, finally leveling out at seventy-five million by the middle of the next century, according to demographers.

But there was worse news than that. In 1989, the wildlife crisis in black Africa seemed to be reaching life or death proportions. Poaching was rampant everywhere, most virulently in East and Central Africa. The black rhinoceros had been virtually exterminated throughout the continent, killed for its horns that could bring up to $50,000 apiece in Asia and the Middle East for drugs or dagger handles, and only about 4,000 rhinos remained in all of Africa. Elephants seemed on the verge of following them into extinction.

As the price of ivory soared from $2.45 a pound in the early 1960s to $100 or more in 1989, elephant numbers tumbled. In a mere decade, they declined from 1.3 million to less than 625,000 in the thirty-six (of forty-four) countries where they remained. Kenya alone had lost eighty-five percent of its herd in the past thirty years—down from 169,000 in 1969 to fewer than 20,000 today. The world market was demanding eight hundred and twenty-five tons of ivory a year, most of it going to Asia where it was worked into jewelry, statuary, and in Japan (which consumed forty percent of it) mainly into *hanko*, the signature stamps that Japanese do business with. The value of raw and worked ivory is about $550 million a year, of which African governments—at least legally—reap only $6 million. But as poachers killed off the mature bulls and cows with the biggest ivory, it became necessary to kill more and more elephants to acquire the 825 tons the market needed—up to 80,000 elephants a year, most of them by now juveniles. According to one monitoring group, the average tusk weight imported to Japan dropped from 35.8 pounds in 1979 to 21.3 in 1982, and by 1989 ivory confiscated in East and Central Africa was averaging about ten pounds.a tusk. Experts began predicting the extinction of the African elephant by the end of the century.

Then Kenya's President Daniel arap Moi, in a bold move for a leader in politically chaotic Africa, ordered poachers shot on sight, and followed up early last year by appointing a white Kenyan, the renowned and controversial paleo-anthropologist Richard Leakey, to head up a new, semi-autonomous combination of the country's parks and wildlife departments to be called Kenya Wildlife Services.

As conservationists called for a worldwide ban on the ivory trade, and the media responded with film and stories of the elephant slaughter, Moi provided the most dramatic footage of all when he torched twelve metric tons of confiscated ivory worth more than $3 million in a symbolic bonfire in Nairobi National Park. It was splendid theater, but to make sure that the fire didn't fizzle and dampen the effect of the propaganda, "special effects" experts painted the two thousand tusks in the eighteen-foot high pyre with highly flammable glue, underlain with plenty of dry kindling and—for added insurance —a grid of gas pipes to fuel the flames. It came off as planned, a fiery gesture of defiance to poachers and traders alike, urging the world to "Ban the Bloody Ivory Trade."

Some critics felt the gesture would have been more meaningful had Moi thrown his signature of office, an intricately carved ivory *rungu* (war-club), into the flames, and that the money realized from the sale of that ivory could have bought a whole lot of modern weapons and transportation for anti-poaching forces. But as Leakey, who dreamed up the bonfire, said: "We weren't going to get public opinion on our side for an ivory ban if we hadn't done something fairly dramatic to demonstrate our commitment."

It worked. In October of 1989, during an emotionally charged meeting at Lausanne, Switzerland, the Convention on International Trade in Endangered Species (CITES) voted to move the African elephant from its Appendix II (threatened species list) to Appendix I (endangered), thus outlawing the ivory trade among its one hundred-three member nations. Tusks could still be taken by sporthunters under strict regulation and oversight, though not for market sale.

But while elephants were being slaughtered by the thousands in East, Central, and West Africa, the nations of southern Africa—principally Zimbabwe, Botswana, South Africa, and recently independent Namibia— have seen their herds thrive. Zimbabwe and Botswana, with more than 100,000 elephants between them, have more now than ever before. The closely managed herds of South Africa, Namibia, and Malawi, numbering 15,000, remain stable. But only because game departments and sport-hunters cull them. In Zimbabwe, landowners (black and white alike) also own the wildlife on their properties, a fact that encouraged them to keep it healthy and make money from shooting safaris. The ivory, meat, and hides culled by the game departments are sold, the profits plowed back into game management and local economies.

Southern Africa saw no reason why its elephants—which without control would soon grow too many and begin destroying habitat both for themselves and other wildlife, not to mention the havoc they could wreak on human populations and agriculture—should fall under a ban brought about by mismanagement, corruption, and rampant poaching in other parts of Africa. In the end, four southern African nations—South Africa, Malawi, Zambia, and Zimbabwe (Namibia is not yet a CITES member)— joined China in filing reservations to the ban. Britain joined them part- way, filing a reservation for Hong Kong until that colony could dispose of the four hundred-seventy tons of ivory it had stockpiled. But in effect the ivory trade is dead, for awhile, at least.

So on the surface anyway, with the ivory ban and the media attention and the slowing of elephant slaughter in East Africa, things seemed to be looking up for African wildlife as 1990 began. But I knew that things are never what they seem on the surface in Africa.

What was really going on? What about the less-glamorous species of wildlife—from Cape buffalos and spotted hyenas and the once-ubiquitous herds of antelopes and gazelles (down to the tiny dik-dik), to the preda- tors, the birds, the snakes, the land itself? What was happening in the vil- lages, among the *wainanche*—the common folk—and their herds?


TO MOST RURAL AFRICANS, wildlife is the enemy—*adui* in Swahili—a destroyer of lives and crops and cattle. It is also a wel- come source of meat in a world always short on supper, thus the prevalence of the wire snare and the poisoned arrow in most rural dis- tricts. Indeed, a single Swahili word, *nyama*, encompasses the concepts of both "meat" and "wildlife." Was the people's attitude toward wildlife changing for the better? Not likely, given that mind-set.

Since the worldwide success of the Kenya-filmed movie *Out of Africa* in 1985, wildlife tourism has become that nation's largest source of for- eign currency—more than 600,000 visitors spent about $350 million in Kenya last year. But the spate of recent deaths, both of elephants and tourists alike, must have had some effect on the popularity of East Africa as a vacation mecca. How were the game parks faring? And for all of Moi's and Leakey's pledges to rid the game department of inefficiency and corruption, was it actually happening?

In six weeks, I covered some 2,000 miles—most of it in four-wheel drive vehicles but the best parts, as always, on foot—and visited nearly twenty national parks, forest preserves, and privately owned game ranches in two countries: Kenya and Tanzania, once the jewels in East Africa's wild crown. I talked with scores of people, black and white and Asian, in at least four languages (English, German, Kiswahili, and Maa, the Nilotic language of the Masai and Samburu tribes among others) ranging from

tribal cattle drovers, government game scouts, park wardens and foresters
through professional hunters, bush pilots, and tour operators, to
European, American, and African tourists, conservationists, wildlife
experts, and government officials, including Richard Leakey, the new
director of Kenya Wildlife Services, and David Babu, Tanzania's director of
National Parks.

The Africa I'd first visited a quarter of a century ago was vast, rich, and
wild—a sprawl of seemingly endless game plains teeming with life and
death, of deserts as hard and cruel and hot as a thousand Death Valleys, of
strong, blue-black mountains footed in lush forest and topped with the
ghostlike silver of equatorial ice and snow, all of it pervaded by the
intense, hot light that does unearthly things to colors. Birds gleamed like
jewels, elephants loomed like skyscrapers through the mirage. Blood
seemed to flow brighter there, and plenty had flowed in the past year
alone. George Adamson, with his wife Joy, the champion of wild lions,
was shot to death by Somali *shifta* near his camp at Kora Rock in northeastern Kenya. A Connecticut woman on a photo safari was killed by
poachers-turned-bandits in a holdup between Tsavo and Amboseli national
parks. As the heat came on from Moi and Leakey—more than a hundred
poachers were shot dead by game scouts in Kenya during 1989—the
poachers turned to robbery, killing at least a half-dozen European tourists
in various incidents. Elephant killings dropped dramatically, from 1,500 in
1988 to only a hundred since Leakey's appointment in April, 1989 to April
of 1990. Following the October ban, the price of ivory tumbled to $10 a
pound or less in Somalia's capital of Mogadishu.

My last safari had been in 1981 and I was eager to return, but fearful of
what I might find. Animal Fair or butcher shop? Or perhaps just a tawdry
Eden trying to mend itself?

I found a little bit of all three, and then some.

The horror stories began on my arrival in Nairobi. Two weeks earlier,
just before Christmas, a woman tourist waiting for her luggage at Jomo
Kenyatta International Airport had noticed three unclaimed wicker fruit
baskets going roundy-round on an adjacent carousel. Foul odors and pitiful mewing noises emanating from them caused her to investigate. Inside
the baskets she found three baby chimpanzees suffering from diarrhea,
severe dehydration, and sheer terror. "Absolutely horrified," she reported
her discovery to Stephen Meacher, chairman of the Kenyan Society for the
Protection and Care of Animals. One of the babies also had pneumonia
and died ten days later, but the surviving pair were placed with Mike and
Linda Garner, a horse trainer and his wife who'd raised orphaned chimps
before.

The Garners live in the Nairobi suburb of Karen, only a block or so from the home of Bill and Barbie Winter, who had organized this latest safari. "You've got to see the chimps," Barbie said. "They look like little old men in diapers." So before pushing off into the bush, we stopped by the Garners house to learn the details.

"They're no more than four months old," Linda Garner told us. The chimps, who'd been named Boo Boo and Grumps, awakened from their afternoon nap and were greedily guzzling their bottles of formula. Cuddled in Linda's arms, they made gurgling, cooing noises just like human infants, all the while flexing their inhumanly long, hairy, pink toes in ecstasy.

"I think they're the youngest chimps anyone's tried to raise independently of their mothers," Linda said. "They were apparently captured in Zaire—after the poacher killed their mother. Stephen Meacher says each captured chimp represents seven or eight dead adults. These were destined for Cairo, where they'd have brought anywhere from $10,000 to $20,000 apiece, either as pets or for medical research or the entertainment industry."

Trade in wild chimps was banned in 1973 when CITES put them on the endangered species list. The U.S.–based Primate Protection League estimates that there are only 100,000 wild chimpanzees left in the world. Jane Goodall, the British primatologist renowned for more than thirty years' work with chimps, warned only the previous November that black-market trade in chimps was still flourishing in Europe, Asia, and the U.S.. As they do with elephant ivory, poachers can easily get around the documentation barrier set up by CITES by bribing corrupt officials, in this case to declare the animals captive bred or "personal effects."

The twenty-four–year-old Egyptian who was shipping Boo Boo, Grumps and their now-dead co-captive to Cairo had no documentation at all, and records at the Nairobi airport showed that he had moved baby chimps through the Kenya capital at least once before. Nonetheless, he was fined only $55 under Kenya's Animal Anti-Cruelty Act for shipping the chimps "in a manner likely to cause unnecessary suffering."

"We'd hoped to throw the book at him," Meacher told reporters after the hearing. But because chimps aren't indigenous to Kenya, they aren't covered by its Wildlife Act, which could have levied stiffer penalties. And after all, as Linda told us, "When the man paid his fine, the magistrate hearing the case said, 'Why cannot this man have his monkeys?' I'm afraid that to him, as to many Africans, one 'monkey' is the same as any other. And none of them count for much."

Three years ago the Garners adopted their first orphaned chimp, whom they named Chimmy, after he'd been rescued by tourists from a meat market in Zaire, where he'd been on sale as the prospective main course for a festive Congolese dinner.

"He was three and a half or four years old when we got him," Linda said. "In other words, weaned. At least we didn't have to give him his bottle every few hours. Mother chimps breast-feed, carry and sleep with their babies until they're three years old or more. And a three or four year old chimp is a handful, I can tell you. Chimmy weighed twenty-five kilos—about fifty-five pounds—and he dominated this household. We finally sent him down to Chumfunshi in Zambia last May, where David and Sheila Siddles have a 2,000-acre Wildlife Orphanage. We'll do the same with these two. Jane Goodall has an eight-year-old female in Tanzania that she plans to send down to Chumfunshi, where we hope she'll adopt Grumps and Boo Boo."

And how did Chimmy fare down in Zambia?

Mike Garner's face fell.

"He was never really accepted by their other sixteen or twenty chimps at Chumfunshi," he said. "One day he was playing by himself near the river and crocodiles grabbed him."

Linda looked away and busied herself with Boo Boo and Grumps. They had finished their bottles and were ready for mischief. Or at least Grumps was. Boo Boo, still a bit shy among strangers, clung to Linda and contented himself by pulling his foster mother's hair. Grumps climbed into my arms, fascinated with my sunglasses, which he immediately grabbed with demolition on his mind. When I grabbed them back—a baby chimp has a hell of a grip—he set to work on my mustache as the next best thing.

"It always ends in heartbreak," Bill Winter said as we drove back from the Garners. "I don't know how many orphaned animals—from antbears to lions to zebras—Barbie and I have tried to raise over the years, but most of them finished tragically. Wild animals belong in the wild, Bwana, as I've told you many times. But we never learn, do we? Our hearts go out to them, despite our better judgment, and we pretend that this time it will be different. We'll just raise them through the hard, early time until they can fend for themselves, then release them into the wild. But there's no real 'wild' left—not much, anyway. They always come to grief. How many lions did George and Joy Adamson raise and release, only to become stock killers? To end up shot by a game scout for their skullduggery, or poisoned by a spoonful of Coopertox cattle dip left in a half-eaten cow carcass—like that young lion we found at Shaba in '78, remember him, Bwana?"

I did indeed. Sprawled on his back among the hot, red rocks, his belly distended, humming with flies, while the vultures who'd led us to him squalled impatiently at our rude interruption of their feast. That was on my third safari with Bill, a month-long swing through Kenya to see what effect the hunting ban instituted the previous year by President Jomo Kenyatta had had on the wildlife situation. It hadn't been good.

Indeed, the rumor mill said that Kenyatta had imposed the ban to keep sport-hunting safaris out of the bush and thus make it easier for poaching gangs—under the protection of government officials who took a sizeable cut of the profits—to clean up on rhino horn, ivory and lesser goodies like buffalo horns, zebra hides and antelope meat. In the course of that 1978 safari, we'd seen ample evidence to support the theory: The hills and game plains I'd hunted with Bill in 1971 and again in 1974 were in many cases nearly empty of wildlife, but studded with reeking carcasses and piles of bleaching bones. Elephants were scarce and easily spooked by the approach of our safari wagon. We saw only one rhino on the entire trip—and that one, a cow with a dinky horn, was galloping madly toward Tanzania, where no doubt she met with a warm, heavy-caliber reception.

We actually caught two poachers red-handed on that trip: one, a young Samburu herdboy in the vicinity of Maralal who had just speared an impala ewe he'd found giving birth in a brush-choked *donga* (gully); the other, a game scout tending the gate at the Masai Mara National Reserve who had hidden a freshly shot impala ram under the bunk in his guard hut. Meat poachers both. Small fry. We didn't turn either of them in. For the herdboy, it would have meant a possible death by beating at the hands of the police, or at least a long sentence in the less-than salubrious conditions of a Kenyan jail cell, where prisoners often wade ankle-deep in their own body wastes. The gate guard had a lot of friends, all carrying .303-caliber Lee-Enfields, and he wouldn't have come along peacefully. Bill recommended a non-interventionist policy, and I gladly concurred.

SHABA IS ONE OF EAST AFRICA'S SMALLER and newer game parks, a fifty-square-mile national reserve established in the 1970s and located on the southern banks of the Ewaso Nyiro River just east of the older, larger, and more popular (at least among the minibus crowd)

Samburu and Buffalo Springs reserves. I'd hunted with Bill along the Ewaso Nyiro in 1974, out of the camp he called Elephant Dung Beach on the north bank, and we'd camped in Shaba itself four years later on a photo safari. We'd found the country "stiff with game"—elephants galore, loads of lions and leopards, family groups of Beisa oryx and Grevy's zebra and waterbuck, plenty of big, ugly, daylight-feeding Cape buffalo, and even a black rhino or two. It was in Shaba, in 1978, that I had my most memorable run-in with elephants.

We were camped at a spring called Funan. One night, as I was reading myself to sleep, I heard a sound like a dozen cement mixers churning beyond my tent wall. It was a herd of some eighty elephants that had come down to the spring to drink. When we stepped out of our tents, they panicked and charged right through camp. The amazing thing was, though they caused the very earth to tremble, they didn't touch a single guy-rope as they passed between the tents. I was curious now, a dozen years later, to see how that herd had fared.

Not well, we found out. Nor had the reserve itself. We flew up to Shaba from Nairobi's Wilson Airport in a chartered Twin-Beech—the rivers on Mount Kenya in spate below our wings from the unseasonably long and heavy rains of December—and landed at a new airstrip. Nearby, where only crocodiles and buffalo once basked, stood a slick, new, Italian-designed game lodge, Sarova by name, replete with free-form swimming pools, air-conditioning, and solar panels that glared like square, silvered cataracts from the thatched roofs (but which provided ample hot water for the showers in every room). There was even an up-to-date cocktail lounge that served passable margaritas, just in case anyone felt lonely for Cancun, I guess.

One of Bill's trusted safari men had driven his safari wagon up to Shaba the day before and met us at the airstrip. This man's name was now Steve Austin, but when I'd met him sixteen years earlier he was named Piringin Ole Lekaran, a skinny, half-starved Samburu herdboy tending scruffy cattle on the Tinga Plateau, far to the west, where we'd come to hunt buffalo. His cousin, a lad named Machyana, was one of Bill's trackers. Piringin (whom we soon nicknamed "Shillingi") helped carry out the meat, hide, and horns of the buffalo I killed that day. I will always remember him toting the severed hoofs up to the truck in the lemon-colored sunset and dipping out bone marrow with a straw, surreptitiously, as if we'd begrudge him this rare treat, his equivalent of guacamole. Machyana and the other trackers smuggled the boy back to camp, then back to Nanyuki, where Bill then lived, and he joined Bill and Barbie's "family."

Barbie had tried to enroll him in school, but since he could neither read nor write he was placed with younger children who made fun of his "outlandish" tribal ways.

"He'd go off to school with his lunch all packed but never show up for roll-call," Barbie told me. "Hide out in the hills or forest all day, then come home. His schoolmates scoffed at his pierced ears and the missing lower teeth that are the sign of backcountry, tribal pastoralists—in case they get lockjaw, they can still sip milk and blood. School just didn't work out for him. It doesn't for many of these rural children who are brought too late into the twentieth century."

Later, watching television in the Winters' home, Shillingi discovered *The Six Million Dollar Man* and took Colonel Steve Austin's name for his own. Tribal Africans change their names quite regularly. "Good thing we didn't have the VCR just then," Bill says. "He might have named himself Conan or Rambo. He was well on his way to becoming a *moran*—a warrior—and they love that violent stuff." But for now, the Colonel is a handsome, friendly, strongly built young man of twenty-five, clad in a smart, green, crisply starched safari uniform, a first-rate driver and tracker, married to his childhood sweetheart from Tinga. He is also the owner of a respectable and growing herd of *ng'ombes* (cattle) and, by God, the father of two healthy children—a far cry from his prospects on the day I first met him on the chill, foggy Tinga Plateau.

In two days of coursing the diatomite plains and grasschoked *luggas* (arroyos) of Shaba—rich game lands only yesterday, it seemed—we saw just six elephants, a few small bands of northern Grant's gazelle (none of them with decent horns), one very pregnant crocodile on the red banks of the Ewaso (where once we'd seen hundreds), a few blue-legged Somali ostriches (ditto), some gerenuk standing on their hind legs to browse, long-necked, in the low thorn trees, and a common waterbuck or two. Now and then a reticulated giraffe would appear in the distance—a gaunt, red derrick stalking the scrublands—only to turn at the sight of us and lumber awkwardly toward the horizon. We saw no Beisa oryx, no lions and, worst of all, no buffalo, though it's possible that those animals were feeding away from the river just now, thanks to the heavy rains of the past few weeks that had greened up the usually arid surrounding countryside. We did see a family of four cheetahs, however, alerted to their presence by the clouds of tan dust thrown up by half a dozen minibuses chasing the long-legged cats through the yellow thorns in hopes of photo ops.

"Crikey!" Bill said, as he watched the chase unfold through his binoculars. "They've separated the mother from her three cubs, and the cubs are trying to sneak back to her. Every time they try to cross the track, another minibus roars up, cameras blazing, and drives them back to cover. A new hunting technique, Bwana. Interdiction by Nikon if ever I saw it."

I watched through my own glasses, elbows braced on the coaming of the roof hatch in Bill's big, dark-green Land Rover safari wagon, known familiarly to the crew as *Simba Kali* ("The Fierce Lion"). The hatches and windows of the white minibuses were crammed with sunburnt faces topped in most cases by brand-new bush hats banded in fake leopard skin, all of them pointing Nikons or Canons or video camcorders every which way. The cheetah cubs cowered under bushes or behind blow-downs, the tips of their tails twitching nervously. Distant babble filled the air. French? Italian? German? Whatever it was, it sickened me.

"Let's get out of here," I said. "I can't stand it."

We drove through thorn scrub down a little-used track to our old campsite at Funan, past the dark, basaltic cairns of old Borana gravesites that stud the plain. The campsite had been little used of late, and the spring where we once swam in crystal-clear water after a day of eating Africa's hot dust was almost entirely silted in. A few empty bottles of Fanta orange drink lay half-buried in the muck. I remembered the elephants of yesteryear, outlined like flapping black storm clouds against the moonlit sky as I poked my head out of my tent. I remembered, too, the long-ago trumpet as they took off, charging through the ancient graves of warriors, their passage marked by clouds of dust that glowed dimly red in the moonlight. There was no fresh elephant sign beside the spring—no big footprints slowly filling with water, no glossy dung piles with butterflies dancing over them, no freshly torn branch scars on the thick, surrounding scrub.

A ghost camp indeed.

"The *shifta* have hit this area pretty hard," Bill said. "Do you remember E.D.B.?"

In 1974, at Elephant Dung Beach, across the Ewaso and about twenty miles downstream toward the town of Merti, the *shifta* were very much evident, even then. Wrecked trucks lined the two-track to Merti, where we'd gone to report our presence in the hunting block. The police post was ringed in barbed wire, with machine-gun towers at all four corners. The whole place smelled so strongly of *bangi* (marijuana) fumes that you could get a contact-high with half a dozen deep inhalations.

"Yes, *shifta* very bad men," the post commander told us, grinning apologetically. "Three hundred of them in this area now, with automatic rifles and plastic explosives to blow up traffic on the road. We have not the strength to fight them, only enough to guard our post. Very bad men."

"But not three hundred of them," Bill said later, during the tense drive back to camp. "Maybe thirty, if that many."

Yet that was enough, I remember thinking as I looked more closely at the wrecks along the road. The frames and sheet metal of the dozen or so lorries and *matatus*—free-lance buses, ubiquitous in East Africa in lieu of public transportation—were ripped and twisted as if by a mad giant's hand, the metal scorched in places by the blast of plastic explosives. *Shifta* had left plenty of signs of their presence around our camp: the tuskless, tattered hulk of an elephant they'd killed nearby, the hacked bones and hide of a giraffe shot for meat. One day while we were out hunting, a half dozen of them, clad in the *kikoys* (sarongs) and ragged *kilembas* (headdresses) of Somalis approached the camp but were driven off by the staff after an exchange of rifle fire. On our way out of E.D.B. at the end of the hunt, only the sharp eyes of our trackers saved us from being blown up: The trackers spotted freshly disturbed dirt in the two-track ahead where a land mine had been planted. We skirted it and got the hell out of there.

Clearly, the *shifta* had worked this area with virtual impunity. The only anti-poaching patrol we met in Shaba on this trip had pulled their lorry just off the road near the lodge at midmorning. In the bed of the truck, trussed and bawling, lay a goat ready for slaughter. The camouflage-clad game scouts had their cutlery and cookpots out and in good order for their accustomed "elevenses." A burly noncom with a G-3 assault rifle at the ready told us to take no photographs. Like those of the others, his uniform was clean and pressed and his boots spit-shined, showing no dust, thorn-snags, or other evidence of foot patrols through the bush. For these lads, antipoaching duty was clearly a picnic.

On our last morning's game drive in Shaba, we encountered a lone bull elephant traveling purposefully through open country. We approached him in Simba Kali with great caution. "These poor chaps have been hammered pretty hard," Bill warned. "They could be mean." But this elephant only looked saddened, gazing down at us almost chidingly as he swung past. "Look at that poor old sod," Bill said. "By rights he ought to turn and pound us for all the pain and grief our kind has wrought on his. But he's forbearing, forgiving, not vengeful at all." He slammed the palm of his hand on the dashboard. "God, what vile beasts we are!"

The elephant's right tusk had been broken off near the root, but the left tusk, though short, was thick—probably thirty-five to forty pounds of ivory there. More than $4,000 worth.

WE HEAD SOUTH AND WEST TOWARD the Samburu-Buffalo Springs game reserves, which, with a combined total of a hundred fifteen square miles, straddle the Ewaso Nyiro north of the frontier town of Isiolo. If our meeting with the one-tusked bull was elegiac in its tone, our first run-in with the elephants of Samburu was downright poignant.

En route to Larsen's, a swank tented camp located in a grove of magnificent, olive-barked yellow thorns (which early settlers called "fever trees" because of their proximity to insect-breeding water, not yet figuring out the connection between bugs and blackwater), we saw an obviously motor-inspired cloud of dust moving rapidly on a collision course with ours. Out of the cloud emerged a band of elephants—no more than twenty of them—closely followed by a brace of safari wagons. The elephants, all adolescents or young adult females with calves, tossed their heads and trunks as they ran, clearly angry at this interruption of their usual midday siesta, during which they stand in the shade digesting their morning's fodder. When they saw Simba Kali in their way, they stopped and milled around, flapping their ears in consternation.

One infant, barely as big as a Volkswagen Beetle, darted out from between his teenaged mother's legs and gave us what for—ears flared, trunk up, showing tusks no bigger than bananas, he stamped his tiny forefeet and trumpeted. Well, *piccoloed* would be more like it. A fierce, high, tremulous bleat like a Tarzan sound track in diminuendo.

Bill honked Simba Kali's horn right back at him. The Fierce Lion—for all its impressive bulk, its custom-built steel-sheeted box body, its three roof hatches, its big-bore Range Rover engine, its two steel-reinforced, deep-treaded spare tires, its side-hung petrol *debes* (jerry cans) and reserve water cans—has a pitifully weak-sounding horn. Our feeble answering squawk broke everyone up in hysterical giggles.

"*Simba Kali,*" intoned Colonel Austin from the rear photo hatch, in his most leonine voice. Then he laughed until tears came to his eyes. Africans love the absurd.

Off-loading minutes later at Larsen's, Bill asked a minibus driver what he had seen, game wise, on that morning's run through Samburu.

"*Ndovu moja,*" the man said. "One elephant. A few safari ants, and maybe a rat." He laughed bitterly and spat in the dust: *Whap !*

We didn't see much more during our two days in the reserves. A lot of dik-diks ("Double Richards" in Bill's old white-hunter parlance), one of them apparently mesmerized by a large snake that our approach frightened off, though the diminutive antelope remained frozen in place, afraid to move for fear that either the snake or Simba Kali would kill him. Many gerenuk. Some crested cranes prancing their mating dances in a grassy plain. A crocodile or three along the Ewaso's mudbanks. A few very shy elephants hidden back in the riverine forest—and much evidence of their destructive feeding habits in the form of uprooted trees and ripped branches near the river itself. And the highlight of our stay: a young, very pale female leopard, not much larger than an ocelot, that sprawled ineffably bored along the limb of a tree overlooking the Ewaso Nyiro while hordes of minibuses maneuvered for position beneath her, and camera shutters chirred like a plague of locusts. Until she moved her head, I wondered if she weren't a stuffed leopard, placed there by the park authorities to satisfy tourist "click-art" appetites. No wild leopard in a hunting block would ever put up with that indignity.

One hot afternoon we stopped at Samburu Lodge for a look-see at the tourist traffic and a little liquid refreshment. The last time I'd visited the lodge, in 1978, it had been packed with bush-jacketed Americans. Now it was virtually empty.

"KATO—the Kenya Association of Tour Operators—says U.S. bookings are down forty percent this year," Bill observed gloomily. "Alas, I fear the bloom is off the East African rose, what with last year's murders and all the publicity given the elephant poaching. At least as far as Americans are concerned. The West Germans and Scandinavians, who came down here in droves for their midwinter 'sex safaris' on the coast, have been scared off by AIDS. I sometimes wonder if that acronym doesn't stand for Africa In Dire Straits. Now the hot tourist venues seem to be the Far East: Thailand, Indonesia, Borneo, even mainland China. Who wants to come here and see dead elephants? Or get plugged by some crazed bandit with a burp gun? And now with Eastern Europe opening up, Africa, I fear, will be left even farther behind."

From Samburu and the Northern Frontier we drove south through Isiolo, once a quiet, sun-baked cowtown reminiscent of the American Wild West. Today it's a teeming Babel of panhandlers, garish tourist shops, hawkers flogging crude wood-carvings and fake, plastic elephant-hair bracelets, all overhung with a greasy miasma of unmuffled diesel exhaust from Kenya's ubiquitous *matatus* that threatens the pristine whitewash of a new, multi-million-shilling mosque (the only attractive building in town). We then hit the pavement, much-patched but still potholed tarmac, toward Mount Kenya. We were headed for Bill's own tented camp, which had been erected in the Aberdare Salient while we "lodged it" at Shaba and Samburu, but first we had to make a side trip to Lewa Downs.

"We've seen a bit of what the public lands have to offer," Bill said. "Now we'll have a look at the private sector." Lewa Downs, Ltd., is a 42,000–acre (sixty–five square mile) cattle and game ranch on the edge of the Laikipia Plateau. More than 2,000 elephants circulate through it and adjacent private ranches—Kenya's largest remaining herd outside of the 8,034-square mile Tsavo National Park, which holds about 5,500 tuskers. We arrived in time for lunch (roast beef, and Yorkshire pudding) with Ian and Jane Craig in their spacious, thatch-roofed home built of local stone and hand-hewn beams atop a breezy bluff with a splendid view. Below, it seemed to me, sprawled the old Africa—miles and miles of game plain rich with acacia-browsing giraffes, mixed bands of zebras and antelope, and riverine forest through which big, black herds of buffalo slowly circulated. The Craigs' eleven-year-old son, Batian (who takes his name from one of Mount Kenya's twin peaks, which in turn is named for a legendary Masai chieftain), had his pet bushbaby, Tikki, perched on one shoulder. During lunch, a number of rock hyraxes poked their fuzzy noses in the French doors to size up the newcomers.

Ian Craig, who worked for Bill during the old hunting days, is coordinator of the Laikipia elephant scheme. "We have one hundred eighty to two hundred elephants living year-round on Lewa," he said, "with a maximum of six hundred forty-five seasonally, when they come down from the Matthews Range. I'd estimate ten to fifteen leopards on the Downs, perhaps as many as three hundred Grevy's zebras—the pin-striped ones, you know, rare now throughout the country—and adequate lion, at any given time perhaps four to six *simbas*. Our giraffe, waterbuck, and Burchell's zebra are abundant, and I hope to crop them commercially when sport hunting reopens, which Richard [Leakey] says will be soon."

How's the poaching situation in the area?

"We get them moving down from the northern boundary of the ranch, which is unfenced," Ian said. "I have sixty-four men working under me, ten of them armed. One five-man anti-poaching team is always on patrol along the northern boundary. Out of a thirty-day month, they're in the bush twenty-six days. They're good men in the bush—Turkana and Wandorobo from the northern tribes, and Wakamba from the *bundu*, the thorn country down around Tsavo, a tribe with a long hunting and tracking tradition. They're all armed with .308s, and I see to it that they each fire 250 rounds on the target range each year. They can shoot, all right."

Ian had recently encountered a *shifta* band in the Matthews Range.

"We were too few, and too poorly armed, to engage them," he said, "so we watched to see how they operated. There were seven of them, all carrying either G-3s or Kalashnikovs. Some wore dark-green, military-style uniforms with long trousers and sleeves, others, a kind of Somali *kikoy* or sarong and the usual *kilemba*-like head cloths. Protection from the sun, you know. We first heard, then saw them firing bursts of full auto for forty-five minutes. The elephants were running, trumpeting and screaming. The *shifta* chased and shot at them over a distance of about three kilometers—nearly two miles—and killed five elephants all told. I don't know how many they wounded. They were all young animals, with fifteen or twenty pounds of ivory to the tusk, maximum. They chopped the tusks out with axes and then carried the ivory to a small copse of extremely dense bush, where we couldn't observe them. You could see they'd had military training. When they crossed open trails, they covered one another and moved very fast, very silently. Three of them were obviously porters, carrying small kit—canteens, *sufurias* [metal cooking pots], sleeping mats, and the like."

"After they'd cleared out, we went into the cover where they'd hidden the ivory. We searched it for two bloody hours—and this with 'Dorobo trackers, mind you, the best in the business—yet we never found a tusk." He shook his head again and grinned wryly. "They're bloody good, I'll tell you!"

After lunch we drove out on a brief swing through the ranch, along the Ngare Sergoi (Zebra River), admiring the rich stand of yellow thorns that flanked its banks. "You don't see many stands of fever trees as mature as these anymore," Bill said. "They make excellent firewood, unfortunately, so they're going fast throughout East Africa."

Across the river, we climbed a long hill through park-like country and came up with a bull elephant out for an afternoon stroll. He raised his trunk and trumpeted twice at us, then, after a few steps in our direction, thought better of it and sloped on down to the river valley. At the bottom of the hill's far side, we met up with one of Ian's recon teams—lean, leathery men who spoke no English, with the pierced, stretched earlobes and alert, bushwise manner of upcountry tribesmen. Their rifles appeared well cared for, no rust on the barrels, the stocks and forends gleaming with hand-rubbed linseed oil. They were headed for a new campsite, patrolling as they went. After exchanging a few words with them, we headed across country to another outpost, paralleling along the way a twelve-foot-high electrified fence.

"The fence both keeps our rhinos—fifteen of them now—from wandering off the ranch, where they'd be killed in no time, and alerts our main headquarters back at the house if anyone tries to cut it or climb it," Ian explained. "It sounds off up to seven kilometers away—better than four miles. Bloody pricey, to be sure, but it's the only way to keep the poor *kifaru* safe from poachers."

We stopped on a windswept lava ridge and walked down to an outpost where three well-armed, uniformed men intently scanned the country below. We could see rhinos moving in the scattered acacias and beyond them, in the more open grasslands, the creamy blotches of grazing eland. The smaller, russet shapes of impala moved among them. "Our impala are nicely balanced now with the carrying capacity," Ian said. "The eland, though, are decreasing. Not through poaching—I think they've reached the limit of what we can carry on Lewa Downs and are in the process of adjusting. You know, Bill, the game is now going the other way. It's a lot better than it was even a year ago. There's a new wave of hope in the country, since the president's shoot-to-kill order and Richard's appointment. Here, we've been protecting the game *hard* now, and it's paying off."

Our final stop at Lewa was at the tidy fieldstone home of Mrs. Anna Merz, an Englishwoman who, with no support from any wildlife conservation organization, has ventured her own money from the goodness of her heart on this fence-enclosed rhino sanctuary. A fit, outdoorsy, no-nonsense woman, she met us at her massively timbered front gate, accompanied by her "Sweetheart," a five-year-old female black rhino named Samia whom Mrs. Merz raised from an orphaned calf.

"Be careful," she warned us. "My Sweetheart is quite jealous. I don't want her tossing you into the trees or crushing you against the fence."

Though Samia's horns were still just nubbins, her bulk was impressive. We capered through the slightly opened gate like so many banderilleros expecting a horn up the backside from an enraged fighting bull.

Over tea and biscuits, we discussed the current climate of Kenya in regard to wildlife. "I think the president has a real, a *sincere,* interest in saving the wildlife and the trees," Mrs. Merz said doubtfully, pursing her lips as if daring anyone to contradict her. "I feel the country is very fortunate to have him for president."

While Boyd went out for a photographic stroll with Mrs. Merz and Samia to take advantage of what was left of the day's light, I went into the bathroom. Mounted over the "facilities" was a framed Gary Larson cartoon showing an elderly couple standing in a hallway perusing a front door through which protrudes a huge, quivering rhino horn. "For heaven's sake, Lee," the woman is saying. "That spoiled rhino is going to either bellow or charge the door all night till we let him in!"

So Anna Merz has a sense of humor. Or does she?

"I hae me doots," Bill said in his best Scottish burr as we drove away at sunset. "When her 'Sweetheart' reaches sexual maturity, Mrs. Merz might find herself up in a treetop with two or three horn holes in her. Or crushed like a lovebug against the craggy bark of a fever tree. You can carry this anthropomorphic business just a tad too far."

We drove direct, largely in the dark, passing through the crowded, almost unrecognizable midden of downtown Nanyuki. I hadn't seen the town in more than a dozen years. I looked away, to the icy twin peaks of Kirinyaga, "The House of God," as Mount Kenya was known of old, wondering what He made of the scene.

We put up that night at Nyeri, in the heart of the Aberdare Range, in the Outspan Hotel—a grand old pile dating back to Kenya's early colonial period at the turn of this century. Lord Baden-Powell, who gave the world the Boy Scouts, once said: "The nearer to Nyeri, the nearer to heaven." Old India hands felt that Nyeri and its cool, green environs were "the Simla Hills of Africa," in reference to the cool Himalayan foothills where the elite of the British Raj spent their summers. Baden-Powell himself is buried on the Outspan's grounds, as is Colonel Jim Corbett, the great hunter-naturalist whose tales of tiger hunting in India, *Man-Eaters of Kumaon* foremost among them, were best-sellers in the United States and Britain just after World War II. Following India's independence in 1947, Colonel Corbett retired to Kenya where he wrote his splendid books. Then died.

Nyeri is the epicenter of Kenya's population quake, with a human growth rate of 4.4 percent (the national average in 1989 was 3.8 percent; the world's growth rate was 1.8 percent). That means, in practical terms, that a Nyeri woman in the course of her child-bearing years will give birth to 8.5 children. Kenya is the world's fastest growing country in terms of human numbers, its population doubling every seventeen years. Nyeri is in the heartland of Kikuyu country. The Kikuyu are the largest of Kenya's thirty-six tribes, with 3.2 million members as of the 1979 census, and about five million today. In procreation, as in politics, the Kikuyu lead the nation. "It's a sacred tradition among the Kikuyu," an ethnologist told me, "for each family to name a child for each of its four grandparents. That means a family minimum of two male children and two female. At those odds, the Kikuyu need no encouragement from the Pope when it comes to overbreeding."

East African men, even among less ferociously fertile tribes, are notoriously macho. Beside them, the Latin lovers of legend—Don Juan, Casanova, Rubirosa—seem like lace-collar poufters. Rape and sexual murder are unfortunately common in Africa, and a Nilotic raider would kill a resisting woman with his *rungu* rather than sully his *mkuki* (spear) with her blood. Steel has magical, masculine powers, easily debased and not to be trifled with. In tribal cultures—the mind-set of which still dominates most African thinking—men rule; women do what they're told or suffer the consequences, often a beating or worse. One of the commonest sights in upcountry Africa, almost a pictographic metaphor to my eye, is of a woman —small, frail, wrinkled, and pancake-breasted, though only forty years old—trudging up some steep, hot, endlessly dusty hill under a load of wood twice or three times her size. Meanwhile the men sit in the village in the shade of a tree, drinking *pombe* (beer) and spinning yarns. When a woman wears out, at least among the nomadic tribes, she is frequently left behind on the trail to die, often with a circle of stone placed around her, as a magical warning to the hyenas not to eat her until she's dead.

Many African women are working for "family planning," and I'm sure most of them desire access to birth control information and devices. Maybe they can change the attitudes of their men, but they'd better do it in a hurry. It may already be too late for Africa's wildlife, crowded out of living space by the flood tide of humanity that's crashed over the continent since independence; judging by the death tolls from famine and disease that have become regular happenings in sub-Saharan Africa over the past decade, it could well be too late for its people.

Such were my gloomy thoughts in Nyeri. They were not brightened the next morning when—prior to occupying our tented camp in the Aberdare Salient—we stopped at a grassy, privately owned airstrip at Mweiga, near Nyeri, to take a glider flight over the area. Spiraling high through the cool, blue mountain air in the yellow-and-white two-seater, I could see two Africas—the old one of lush rainforest and distant savannahs, and the impending new Africa, all tin roofs, maize fields, crowded towns, and clearcuts, held together by a slipshod lacing of frayed tarmac roads, with plumes of blue-gray smoke rising from the areas where charcoal burners were at work; the new encroaching ever more insistently on the old: Yeats' rough beast slouching toward Bethlehem. It occurred to me that, had gliders been available in the early 1880s, one might have viewed a similar scene along the Rocky Mountain Front—but the blue-gray smoke would have bloomed from the muzzles of Sharps .45-110 buffalo rifles, and the campfires of the hidemen....

Colonel Austin took the last ride in the glider. I saw him waiting for the jerk of the winch-driven cable that would lift the bird into the sky, grim-faced in anticipation of the unknown, saw the glider rise gracefully and turn in its widening gyres under the able pilotage of a *mzungu* wind-freak named Richard Pollard, then sweep in for its landing. Steve was relaxed and beaming—as delighted with the flight as he'd been sixteen years earlier at the sight of my dead buffalo.

*"Wewe iko hodari,"* I told him as he clambered out of the cockpit. "You are indeed brave."

*"Iko tamu"* he said, grinning. "It is sweet. But now we must pay money for it!"

I'd seen the green canvas of Bill's tents winking up at me from the forest as we flew, familiar and evocative of good memories, but getting there was even better. Aberdare National Park, established in 1948, comprises three hundred eleven square miles of rainforest and moorland on an isolated volcanic massif that forms the eastern wall of the Great Rift Valley. Shaped like a giant boomerang with a salient on its convex side facing toward Mweiga, it is anchored north and south by two impressive peaks: Lesatima (13,020 feet) and Kinangop (12,815 feet), usually shrouded in swirling clouds. Today both stood clear, as if welcoming us to our camp midway between them.

The peaks swoop down to a vast moorland dominated by giant lobelias, heather, and tussock grass tall as a man. St. John's wort and groundsel grow thick and tall, far bigger under the equatorial sun and high-altitude ultraviolet light than any temperate-zone gardener could imagine. Below timberline the ancient forest—mainly cedars and hagenia—is eerie: shrouded often in clammy mists, the trunks and gnarled branches festooned with a form of Spanish moss called Old Man's Beard.

This area is rich in Kenyan history, most of it grim. As the Kikuyu homeland (they called it *Nyandarua*, "The Drying Hide," after its crusty, wrinkled silhouette), it was the scene of many intratribal wars and bloody battles with plains-dwelling Masai raiders. Then, less than a century ago, British colonialists took over much of the Aberdares as "The White Highlands," confining the tribes to reservations much as Americans did the Indians and establishing plantations of coffee, tea, vegetables, and pyrethrum while logging the virgin hardwoods extensively. On the western slopes lay "Happy Valley" (now Wanjohi), infamous in the 1920s and '30s for the excesses of the *White Mischief* crowd. When Mau Mau erupted in the early 1950s, the giant caves, bamboo thickets, and moorlands of

the higher elevations provided a strategic hideout for Kikuyu "freedom
fighters" and terrorists, as did the forests of Mount Kenya farther to the
east. R.A.F. bombing raids and incursions of the highlands by "pseudo-
gangs" of whites in black-face makeup, disguised as Mau Mau and carrying
concealed Sten guns, failed to dislodge the rebels. I was present in 1964
when the last Mau Mau gang surrendered in Meru, on Mount Kenya, to
officials of the new African government. They were a scruffy, cocky lot, I
recall, dressed in rags and hides and looking less like noble freedom fighters than highway robbers, which is what they'd become, much to the new
government's embarrassment.

Poaching had been light in the park, John Muhanga, the senior park
warden, told us that morning at Mweiga. In the afternoon we took a
game run to see for ourselves. Colobus monkeys abounded along the
rain-rutted, overgrown *njias* (roads), swinging perilously through the
upper canopy in frightening leaps to their branches like potbellied
Tarzans in black-and-white fur coats. Colobus monkeys have been hit
hard by fur-poachers over the years, but these seemed unfrightened by
human observers—a good sign that Muhanga's estimate of the poaching
situation was correct.

We saw many elephants ambling along the roads. One, an adult cow,
had a horribly split trunk tip. "From a cable snare," Bill said, shaking his
head sadly. "Probably set by some meat-poacher for buffalo or giant forest
hog, and she got her *mkono* (her "hand" as the Africans call the tip of an
elephant's trunk) caught in it instead. More wildlife is lost to wire and
cable snares in Africa each year, I'm sure, than to poachers' rifles in a
decade. Before the white man came, the *watu* (people) made their snares
of woven grass, bark, hides, or lianas, but they weren't strong enough to
hold big beasts like buff, rhino, or elephants. Now it's all nylon rope, old
electrical or telephone wire, barbed wire, and woven cables salvaged from
mines or sawmills or construction sites. I've seen snares strong enough to
hold a Centurion tank."

Heading back to camp, Bill sidetracked Simba Kali onto a jungle-
choked, twin-rutted trail that unexpectedly took us into a low, swampy
country full of giant forest hogs, the largest and rarest of Africa's wild
pigs—standing more than three feet high at the shoulder and weighing
up to five hundred pounds.

They weren't described by science until 1907, when that keen hunter-
naturalist, Captain Richard Meinertzhagen of the King's African Rifles, sent
the first specimens to the British Museum. Large-headed and small-eared,
with manes of jet-black bristles down their high-rumped backs and big,

swollen excrescences on their faces, they looked in the green, subaqueous light of the rainforest like creatures from a sci-fi movie. "Meiner" had killed them with a 6.5 mm Mannlicher, and as we watched the hogs feeding sedately in the dusk I thought how easy it must have been to drop them, once he came up on them, even with so light a bullet in such heavy cover. I would have had no desire to kill animals as naive as these, I thought self-righteously, even as wicked as they look. But Meinertzhagen probably excused himself because he was "collecting" for the sake of science.

Then a second, kindlier thought struck me: How hard it must have been for a European sportsman, highly imbued with the sense of "fair chase," to gun down innocent, almost Edenic animals in situations such as this. How could they take pride in the stalk, with the prey totally unworried by their approach?

THE ABERDARES, BOTH MOORLAND AND FOREST, are home to many melanistic species and genetic "sports," perhaps because of the intense ultraviolet radiation the highlands are exposed to— black elephants, black bushbuck, black leopards, and serval cats and genets are common, and Kikuyu legend insists that dark-spotted lions prowl the Nyandarua. I'd love to hunt one of them. The giant forest hogs paid little attention to us as we drove slowly through the small herd, a good sign that they hadn't been heavily harassed by either poachers or tourists. Dense forest and wet, treacherous roads discourage both activities.

"Not for long, though, the way things are going," Bill gloomed. "In a few years, I wouldn't be surprised to see this *njia* marked with a sign saying 'Hog Highway.' That is, if the forest is still standing. With the human population growing at the rate it is, all these trees could go for firewood, charcoal, lumber, and exotic hardwood sales, to Japan or elsewhere, with the newly cleared land being opened to the *wainanchi* for agriculture." About eight percent of Kenya's land area—17,127 square miles of a total 225,000—is currently set aside as wildlife conservation areas, with an equal additional amount gazetted as forest reserves. Judging by what we'd seen of the population explosion at Nyeri that morning, government leaders now, and increasingly in the future, must be sorely tempted to give all or most of that land to the people. In the end, they may have no other choice—and that will be the end for wildlife.

The next morning we visited Solio Ranch, another private spread, this one amounting to one hundred twenty square miles, where a wealthy, reclusive American named Courtland Parfet is attempting to save the endangered rhinoceros. Hard by the Aberdares park, Solio currently holds a fenced population of sixty-one black rhinos and a few whites (which were not native to Kenya but were imported originally from South Africa). We saw rhinos everywhere on the twenty-square-mile fenced portion of the ranch, along with an abundance of lions, impala, buffalo, oryx, Burchell's zebra, and Thomson's gazelle feeding on the lush red oat grass of the plains or dozing through the heat of the day in the yellow thorn forest of the Moyo River.

"I pleaded with Court Parfet to establish a private game reserve here as long ago as the early 1960s, when I was the game warden in this area," Bill said as we stopped to watch nine placid rhinos, one with a long, thin, crowbar-like *pembe* that he estimated to be thirty inches, posed against the skyline. "Thank God he has, the way things have gone. The ranch now actually produces surplus rhinos, which are auctioned off to other private rhino sanctuaries or given to the government for stocking in parks and reserves where they've been wiped out by poachers."

There seems little doubt that the black rhino can be fully reestablished throughout its remaining East African range, if only the predations of poachers, often working in collusion with corrupt government game officials, can be halted. But the price fetched by rhino horn —as costly per ounce nowadays as gold—is a hard lure to overcome. At those prices, anyone could turn poacher. Men commit murder for less every day, and not just in Africa.

We'd been told at the ranch headquarters to rendezvous at noon with a ranch hand named Julius at a stock pond across the Moyo. Clearing a rise, we saw the pond below us and a truck parked nearby. Must be our man. But as we drove down, the truck suddenly turned and sped away, disappearing into the bush in a cloud of red dust. When we arrived at the place where it had been parked, we were momentarily dumbstruck.

There on the trampled earth lay the massive hulk of a dead white rhino, its stumpy legs in the air, the gray hide abuzz with flies. The horns had already been taken—carefully cored out, leaving raw red cavities. No vultures had gathered yet, and we noticed no stench from the body, though the strong wind blowing may have kept it down, so I assumed it was a fresh kill.

"We could be in peril here," I said, thinking that if the truck had contained poachers, not Julius, they might have left a rifleman in the brush nearby, or might soon return themselves.

Images of ambush....

Bill put Simba Kali in gear and floored it.

"Bastards!" he gritted. "Let's get back to the ranch office and report this."

Oh, yes, they told us at headquarters. A bull rhino had drowned in the pond a few days before, miring himself as he chased a hippopotamus. This morning a crew had been sent out to pull the body from the pond, lest it poison the water in its decomposition. About that time, the truck we had seen pulled into the compound. The Africans in it seemed quite unruffled. They were ranch hands, and among them was the long-sought Julius. They had removed the horns to prevent "others" from doing so.

I measured the rhino's longer forward horn—three hand spans, roughly twenty-seven inches. A rhino-horned Djambia dagger can fetch $15,000 in North Yemen, and a good daggersmith could certainly carve two handles from this horn. Dried rhino horn, ground by Asian druggists into fine powder, can be worth $30,000 a kilogram, or more than $850 an ounce. I hefted the longer horn and it felt like ten pounds. Some quick mental arithmetic—$136,000? But I didn't know what the horn would weigh when dried, so that speculation was worthless. Also, the poachers would receive only a fraction of the horn's worth once it reached Asia.

The demeanor of the Africans who'd removed the horns was such as to convince me they were telling the truth. They also convinced Bill, which was more important. We'd witnessed the end of a common African tragedy, he insisted, a death by drowning of a big, cranky animal with poor eyesight that had spotted another big animal—probably the hippo we'd seen—and mistaken it for one of his own kind. He'd chased it into the pond, got mired in the muck. *Na kwisha*—he was finished.

Later we went back to the carcass and photographed it from all possible angles. A tragic sight, symbolic of Africa's way: here today, gone tomorrow. Death has many doors to let out life, and Africa more than most. *Sic transit gloria* rhino.

The following day, enroute to Lake Nakuru National Park, we visited another private game reserve, the 100,000-acre Laikipia Ranching Co., Ltd., located on the arid plateau north of Thomson's Falls. The ranch, Ol Ari Nyiro, is owned by a gracious, green-eyed, honey-blonde Venetian woman named Kuki Gallmann, whom Africa has treated most ungraciously. A sophisticated urbanite who'd married a wealthy Italian industrialist, Paolo Gallmann, she came out to Kenya in 1972 with him, not knowing what to expect. She got body blows: First, her brother-in-law was killed by an elephant he'd wounded while hunting; then Paolo died in a car crash while driving back from the Coast one night; and in 1983, while she was pregnant with her daughter, Sveva, her sixteen-year-old son, Immanuele, a snake fancier, was bitten by a puff adder he was handling and died in her arms.

"If I was meant to leave Africa," she told us over coffee, in her cool, well-appointed living room, "I'd have left then." Instead, she founded the Gallmann Memorial Foundation, devoted to the salvation of the forty-six black rhinos and three hundred to a thousand elephants that range her vast property seasonally, along with six thousand cattle and sheep. There are fifty–two dams on the ranch, providing "stock tanks" for animals, both wild and domestic, and well-armed patrols, as at Lewa Downs, to guard against poachers. Fences further guard the rhinos.

Mrs. Gallmann drove us out to a favorite spot of hers, a steep gorge called *Mkutano* (The Meeting Place) leading down to the Rift Valley far below. A lone, windwarped fig tree, its roots bedded deep in a small, seeping spring, overlooked the gorge. "I call this 'The Tree Where Man Was Born,'" she said. "We've found stone artifacts in the gorge, many of them, and there are many sheltering caves down there. It's awesome, in the old sense of the word, to think that I am part of a continuity in this place dating back to the Pleistocene and earlier. One in which humankind and wildlife shared this place, indeed the entire planet at one time, in mutual harmony. I'm doing what I can to keep it that way, at least here."

On the way back to the manor house, we stopped at a stock tank to watch some elephants drinking. Accompanied by the ranch's chief game scout, a wrinkled Borana tribesman named Hussein Omar carrying a .458 Winchester just in case, we hiked in through sand and thorns downwind of the elephants. One of them spotted us anyway. A big bull in *musth*, with secretions from the glands on his temples staining his face and indicating his state of angry sexual excitement, he flared his ears, raised his trunk to trumpet angrily, then tucked the trunk low on his chest and started toward us.

"He's *mkorofi*—mad as hell," said Bill. "Get ready to run."

Hussein raised the rifle.

The bull pounded toward us, moving much faster than seemed possible for his bulk.

But Bill clapped his hands sharply, three times, and the elephant stopped—not more than fifteen feet away. He raised his trunk and trumpeted once again, shrilly, yet this time almost quizzically, baffled, then turned and went back to the others.

Hussein Omar lowered his rifle, looking somewhat disappointed.

How did Bill do that?

"An old bushman's trick," Bill said, grinning as we walked back to the truck. "It works ninety-nine times out of one hundred. But that hundredth time it's good to have a rifle backing you up. Most elephant charges are bluffs, and the old nineteenth-century English sporting books are full of charging 'tuskers' shot dead in a cloud of dust at the 'last possible moment' by the breathless yet unflappable narrator. If they'd only clapped, they more often than not could have saved themselves the gunpowder. But it makes a much better tale the other way, doesn't it, Bwana? And clapping doesn't provide much in the way of a trophy."

Pushing on to Nakuru that evening, we passed long chains of women carrying firewood out of the roadside forests, trucks loaded with burlap bags of *makaa* (charcoal) heading for market in Nairobi, and dozens of *matatus*—smoky, bald-tired, and laden with happy commuters—bearing such sprightly names as Rainbow Warrior, Tolerance of Ladies, The Early Bird Flying Eagle, and, my favorite, God Is Great: He's Back In Action.

Would that it were so.

OSTRICHES ARE SOMEHOW WILD," the young African said, smiling weakly and still breathing hard. He'd just been chased by an irate pair of them down a muddy, potholed road at the north end of Lake Nakuru National Park while walking to work at the Rhino Rescue Trust compound. We drove him the rest of the way to spare him further peril.

"That must have been Peter and Sara," Jock Dawson chuckled when we told him about the incident. "Those *mbuni* (ostriches) are the most dangerous animals in the park. They've already beaten up two or three rangers and a Japanese birdwatcher, sent them to the hospital." Jock is manager of Rhino Rescue's eighty-six–square-mile sanctuary in Nakuru Park, where twenty-one rhinos (twenty black and one white) currently reside behind forty-five miles of twelve-strand electrified fence. The sanctuary—first of its kind in Africa—was established in July 1987, with a nucleus of nineteen rhinos acquired from elsewhere in Kenya, which had seen its rhino population drop from 20,000 in 1970 to a mere 400 due to rampant poaching. The London-based Trust spends about $4,000 a month to maintain the high-voltage haven.

Jock, a portly, pipe-smoking former hunter in his sixties with white hair and shaggy eyebrows, sipped the tea his companion, a cozy, white-haired woman named Enid, had served us in the living room of their stone cottage. Shallow, alkaline Lake Nakuru sits sweltering in the heart of the Rift Valley, but in the cottage we could have been in the Cotswolds, by the look of it.

"Nakuru's famous for its flamingos, of course," Jock said, "a quarter of a million of them at present, along with an equal number of white pelicans and wintering European storks. But there's plenty of game here besides birds and rhinos. About five thousand head each of waterbuck and impala, one thousand five hundred buffalo, some seven hundred warthogs, and one hundred Rothschild's giraffes. The giraffe herd grew from an original band of twenty-one brought here from Soy, back in 1974 or '75, and we have the capacity for them to double in numbers easily. The fence keeps the game from wandering out of the park and raiding people's *shambas,* but we've got the beginnings of a problem with an overabundance of baboons and vervet monkeys. I've seen the baboons dive right through the electrified fence, and some of them sit right on the top wire, seeming to get what might be called a 'kick' out of it." He chuckled.

As elsewhere, the main threat to the future of the park is human over-crowding. Four rivers once flowed into Lake Nakuru, two of them seasonal, from the Mau Escarpment on the west, but intense settlement on the scarp has short-stopped most of the water. The yellow thorn forest has been scalped for firewood, and now tin roofs rule where once trout streams flowed and big, shy, forest-dwelling bongo roamed.

"The *watu* going to take every square inch of land for themselves eventually," Jock predicted. "The private ranches will go. Perhaps they can save a few parks in the long run, but they won't be as they are now. Oh, there's much brave talk about controlling the birthrate, but not much sign of it yet."

"Many persons concerned about the future of wildlife had high hopes for AIDS at first," Enid chimed in with a sad smile. "It seemed a kind of *deus ex machina*, cruel as it is to say so, that would solve Africa's over-population problem. But I'm afraid it's not to be. AIDS can't catch up with the birthrate, and there's evidence that the disease or some variant of it has been at work, in East Africa at least, for a long, long time."

(We heard similar statements from "rural"—ie. tribal—Africans in both Kenya and Tanzania: "Ah yes, Slim," one old graybeard told us, "my grandfather had it back in the old days, he was very *mgonjwa* [sick] for a long while, but then he got over it. He only died last year." In East Africa, AIDS is called "Slim," because that's what you get when you got it.)

We circled the lake in Simba Kali later that day, admiring the vast, ever-shifting masses of birds but lamenting the poor condition of the water-buck and impala—evident in their patchy "staring" coats and subnormal size—which Jock had told us was due to worms and a deficiency of cobalt and copper in the lakeside forage. In the late afternoon we watched a leopard—one of thirty or forty resident in the park—stalk a pair of sparring impala rams for nearly half an hour. He'd gotten to within charging range when a gawky Rothschild's giraffe walking close to the duellists brought them to their senses and they fled.

"Bloody hell!" said Bill, putting down his binoculars. "I thought for certain we'd see a kill. You know, in all the years I've spent in the bush I've never seen a leopard actually bring down and finish an animal. Perhaps now I never will."

Driving back to our camp at dusk, we passed one stream that was still flowing, though sluggishly, into the lake. The black, slow water was thick with green scum, raw sewage, pop bottles, and worn-out shoes—the garbage of nearby Nakuru Town, wending its way to join the flamingos.

"There's some peripheral poaching, to be sure, but poaching's not our problem here," David Round-Turner said. "People are our problem."

It was getting to be an ugly refrain. A former district commissioner, Round-Turner is a tall, lean, laid-back Kenya citizen who now serves as senior conservation and wildlife advisor to the Narok County Council, the assemblage of Masai elders that administers the seven hundred-fifty–square-mile Masai Mara National Reserve, Kenya's most famous tourist destination. Perhaps too famous for its own ecological good.

"There are six lodges or tented camps inside the reserve and seven outside," David continued. "All of them highly profitable. The lodges want to stay open year round, granting no respite to the habitat, and there's little chance of making them close." As a result, minibuses full of European, American, and Asian game watchers criss-cross the fragile terrain constantly, in ever greater numbers, cutting their own tracks when the designated roads don't take them to the animals they've spotted. "It's the cowboy element that does the damage," David said. "We've had cheetah cubs run over by minibuses. We have only four Suzuki Sierras, donated by the World Wildlife Fund, to patrol against this harassment. Recently we closed an area near Musiara because a cheetah was raising four cubs there. But if the minibus drivers know our patrols are elsewhere, they drive in quite brazenly. There's the possibility of a big tip in it for them."

Round-Turner, an old friend of the Bill's, had dropped by our camp at the base of the Aitong Hills for lunch. Bill had "pioneered" *Kampi ya Kondoo* (The Sheep Camp, so named because he usually bought a sheep from a nearby Masai *manyatta* for the camp staff to eat) some years ago.

It was a pleasant, shady spot beside a small stream, and every night we were serenaded by lions, leopards, hyenas, jackals, and baboons, hunting or hiding in the narrow belt of riverine woodland.

Driving into the camp from the town of Narok, I was dismayed by the changes I saw since I'd last camped in the Mara. Miles and miles of wheat now stood where once Bill and I had watched a herd of about eight hundred buffalo cross the road. *Manyattas* with more roofs of tin or plastic sheeting than of the traditional dried cow dung had proliferated. On our game run that morning, watching from a ridge beneath a giant acacia tree, we'd counted seven gaudy hot-air balloons roaring their dragon's fire over the plain, the wild herds fleeing frantically beneath them, while pursuit vehicles zoomed after them, paying no regard to the roads.

"The boundaries of the reserve were set in 1961," David said, "but there's been a constant nibbling at the edges, like mice, ever since. You couldn't fence the entire reserve—it's too big—but a fence along the eastern boundary would keep the Masai cattle out, and that would certainly be beneficial. But fences are anathema to the Masai."

What about the hot-air balloons?

"They're turning the Mara into Disneyland," Round-Turner said. "At present, there are fifteen of them licensed to fly here—the most I've seen in the air at one time was ten. Richard [Leakey] would like to reduce the number to about ten all told. There's no question that the burners do disturb and distress animals, especially elephants and rhinos, which can't by their anatomical structure look up to see what's casting that giant shadow and roaring like a thousand *simbas*." He leaned back in his canvas chair at the lunch table and drank the last of his postprandial coffee. Then he laughed. "Sometimes I feel like throwing myself into the Mara River and drifting down to Lake Victoria, babbling all the way like Ophelia.

"But look at it from the park-income side. The balloon operators charge two hundred fifty dollars per person for a flight that lasts from twenty minutes to an hour, depending on wind and lift conditions. Each balloon can carry, say, eight passengers. If a dozen balloons fly two hundred days a year, that's four point eight million dollars per annum, of which the reserve gets a goodly share."

The point was clear. Richard Leakey has often said that wildlife in Africa must pay its own way or perish. Much as he might dislike the bad effects of ballooning in the Mara, it certainly does help pay the costs of maintaining a viable reserve.

For now, the Mara's twenty-five rhinos (which are expecting at least three calves this year), 1,200 elephants, 8,000 buffalo, and a "guesstimated" five hundred to six hundred lions seem secure, not to mention the myriad other species from dik-diks to Masai giraffes that swarm the Mara's hills, swamps, and grasslands. But the Mara is only the small northern lobe of the vast Serengeti Plain, 10,000 square miles of which lie below the Kenya border with Tanzania. "There are no rhinos left in the northern Serengeti," Round-Turner told us "and very few elephants. The way the Kuria tribe along the border has been meat-poaching, you'd be hard-pressed to find anything larger than a cane rat down there."

We'd be heading down to Tanzania soon—though not to the Serengeti—and would see how the winds were blowing in that Socialistically impoverished country. Our four days in the Mara, however, were full of wildlife and virtually empty of minibuses (thanks to the heavy rains of year's end, which made four-wheel-drive *de rigueur* in our area). A topi antelope—The Beast with Five Colors, as it's known to the Masai—balanced on every other anthill, it seemed, and a sizable number of wilde-beest, holdovers from the previous seasonal migration, cavorted madly through the lush, sprouting grass. Cheetah seemed unusually abundant and not at all shy.

Late one afternoon we came upon fourteen lions ranging from faintly spotted, half-grown cubs to a heavily maned *dume* (male), feeding on a freshly killed giraffe. They too appeared tranquil. Elephants roamed everywhere, some of them short-tempered. One morning at dawn we watched eight horsemen—"One of Tony Church's equestrian safaris, no doubt," Bill said—approach a lone bull across an otherwise empty plain, until a sudden false-charge by His Majesty sent them galloping out of harm's way. Later that morning we came upon a pair of spotted hyenas in the act of mating—a sight never before vouchsafed to Bill the Old Bushman in all his years a-wandering.

The rarest encounter, though, because of the recent decline in their numbers, was with a family of Cape hunting dogs. We came upon the pups first, six of them about five or six months old in Bill's estimation, resting in the middle of an empty short-grass intervale. *"Mbwa mwiti,"* Bill said. "Wild dogs. The parents must be off hunting some breakfast." Sure enough, a few minutes later three adults came trotting back, two of them males wearing radio collars, the female uncollared. The pups ran out to meet them, yipping and squeaking eagerly like outsized mice. They came back bearing some muddy intestines and the head of a Tommy ewe, whereupon a tug-of-war ensued for the best portions.

On our final evening a sudden rainstorm—unusual but welcome for this season—swept down on us from a pewter-colored sky. Around us the low, gray whistling thorns set up an ominous piping in the wind. A big band of impala, joined by nine giraffes, stood with their backs to the storm. There were no other vehicles in sight. For a moment I felt I was back in the old Africa.

I F THE MARA HAD PROVIDED A TASTE of the Edenic past (though a bit frayed around the edges), our next stop, at Amboseli National Park near Mount Kilimanjaro, boded poorly for East Africa's wildlife future. Amboseli was the first African game park I'd visited, back in 1964, and I remembered it as a green vista covered with plains game, elephants, and cantankerous rhinos—too many for comfort, sometimes, with their penchant for charging every vehicle that passed close to their cover. Now the nearest rhino is a hundred miles away, and seven hundred-thirty elephants who've crowded into the park to escape poachers threaten to reduce its 1,259 square miles to desert.

Game lodges have sprouted and grown old in the acacia groves where once I slept under green canvas and was awakened at dawn by the pink glow of sunlight on the eternal snows of Kilimanjaro, only to see giraffes browsing the thorn-tops a few yards from my tent. Now trees knocked down by feeding elephants lie like broken black skeletons in the heart of the park, and dust devils whirl angrily over barren salt pans. The only things moving faster and kicking up more dust than the whirlwinds are the hordes of minibuses, many equipped with two-way radios, that swoop down like motorized vultures on any lion or cheetah innocent enough to wander near a road. The desiccated skulls of an elephant and a mossy-horned wildebeest flank the door of the park office, where a sign rightly warns: "Please Be Careful of Cigarettes." Lung cancer be damned, it's the risk of fire that's too high—even after a Noatically wet December.

Prowling the park in Simba Kali, we passed Lookout Hill, an abrupt knob rising from the flats, topped by a pay telescope and a thatch-roofed, opensided sun shelter resembling a refreshment stand. A deeply eroded trail led up one side, and minibuses parked thick at the base.

"Hot dogs on the left, Häagen-Dazs on the right, postcards and condoms straight ahead," Bill said wearily. "It's the wave of the wildlife future."

More minis trailed off to the east, dragging roostertails of beige dust behind them. Everywhere we looked were elephants and vehicles. One big bull caught our attention. He was limping along at a goodly clip, haloed in birds that swooped and hawked for the insects stirred up by his passage. He was tossing his head angrily.

"Christ,it looks like his left hind leg has been girdled with an axe,"Bill said as we got closer. "He's been in a cable snare. If any elephant has a right to be angry,he does. But still,it looks like it's healed well. We'll ask Cynthia."

We were looking for Cynthia Moss,the American zoologist who has studied Amboseli's elephant herd for more than twenty years and whose book *Elephant Memories* is among the best popular accounts of their ways. We found her finally at the edge of an alkaline marsh in a faded blue tent,tucked away in the bush far from the lodges. "That's Harmon," she said of the crippled elephant,pouring us warm beer in the shade of her tent fly. "He had a wire snare around his leg awhile back,cinched tight. The vets came down from Nairobi and darted him so we could cut it away and shoot him full of antibiotics. He's okay now,but he'll always have a limp."

A short,compactly built woman,middle-aged with brownish-blonde, curly hair,Cynthia spends four or five days a month in Amboseli. Her tent is complete with a bookcase—heavy on Shakespeare and Dick Francis, Margaret Drabble and Raymond Chandler. One title that caught my eye was Ferdinand Celine's macabre *Death on the Installment Plan*. It prompted a question: Aren't Amboseli's seven hundred-thirty elephants more than the park's carrying capacity?

"I hate that term,"the zoologist snapped,shaking her head like the testy Harmon. "Look,the elephants are doing fine right now. The relation-ship between elephants and trees is a very complex one. If you're sug-gesting that they should be 'cropped' as they are in Zimbabwe and South Africa,I suggest they should have more protection from the government game rangers so they don't have to stay huddled near the lodges for fear of getting gunned down by ivory-poachers or speared by young Masai try-ing to prove their manhood." She paused to catch her breath....

Enough said.

"But doesn't Richard Leakey promise better protection?"Bill asked.

"We'll see,we'll see."

Careful,Bill,I thought. She seemed so defensive about her elephants that I expected her at any moment to sprout tusks and a trunk and,like a protective matriarch,grab anyone who crossed her path and fling him through the tent wall. We took our leave shortly,Cynthia coming out with us to stand among the skulls of dead elephants—collected posthu-mously for aging studies—that were arrayed on the campground and expatiating on the differences in philosophy between the southern and East African wildlife management policies.

"In southern Africa,when you get right down to it,"she said,"the approach is more like ranching. They drill boreholes,build dams,and basically see the animals as a cash crop,much like cattle. East Africa,on the other hand,is trying to keep the habitat natural—forever wild,hands off,let it burn,et cetera—as Americans do in wilderness areas and national parks. The southern Africans are more like the U.S.Forest Service,practicing intensive management for sustained yield. There's something cold and heartless about that."

It occurred to me that Richard Leakey's approach to wildlife—his stated intent to reopen high-priced sport hunting,his promise to share tourism revenues directly with the local tribes involved,and especially his insistence that "wildlife must pay its own way"in Kenya's future—more closely resembled southern Africa's than that of,say,Cleveland Amory's or PETA's. But certainly Cynthia Moss wouldn't care to hear that. She might grow tusks....

We returned to our camp in the roseate glow of yet another spectacular Kilimanjaro sunset. A postcard-perfect evening. Pink elephants everywhere. A bucket-shower,the water heated over the cook fire,would be waiting to sluice away the day's crusting of alkaline dust. Then drinks beside the campfire—there's a lovely phrase in Swahili,*kuota moto*,to dream by the fire,which captures the essence of this fine safari moment—before another of our estimable camp cook,Lord Hair's,magnificent four-star repasts. I'd noticed that His Lordship always concocted enormous portions of every delicacy he prepared.

"Yes,"Bill concurred, "because the lads get to polish off the leftovers. I'm sure that as soon as we leave on a game run in the morning,they all gather to decide the menu for the day. 'Let's see,how about a nice lobster bisque to start,loads of fresh asparagus vinaigrette,a roast leg of lamb— not too much garlic,mind you—and fresh strawberries in Devonshire clotted cream to finish? But be sure you prepare enough! The *mzungus* might eat more than their share.'"

I certainly agreed with that last. We'd need all the strength we could muster during the coming week. Tomorrow we were plunging south,into darkest Tanzania.

I REALLY DON'T LIKE TANZANIA. Most of my experiences in that bastion of black African Socialism had involved long,fruitless waits in government offices for appointments that never came off;tiresome,exhausting hassles with arrogant petty bureaucrats;bad food,worse roads,telephones that never worked,and the demeaning but endlessly necessary payment of *chai*—literally "tea," but actually a euphemism for bribe money. In that sense, *chai* is Africa's universal solvent. Everything you wanted to do in Tanzania seemed to require the sullen thwack of at least ten rubber stamps, and the man wielding the ninth was always out to lunch. If I had a dime for every dollar wheedled or just plain stolen from me in Tanzania, I might not be able to retire tomorrow, but I could certainly afford a vacation in Bora-Bora.

Amazingly this time, our trip through the twilight zone at Namanga border post the following morning went without a hitch. Part of that was because Tanzania in 1984 had found itself flat on its economic butt, after seventeen years of former President Julius K. Nyerere's ruinous *ujamaa* ("villagization") policy, which had forced the resettlement of some nine million Tanzanians into "communal" villages in the boondocks and led to enormous losses in agricultural production—which affords a living of sorts to eighty-five percent of the populace. By tightening its belt and "restructuring" *ujamaa*, the country won back some of the needed foreign aid—mainly from Scandinavian countries—it had lost. ("We're trying to get Tanzania back to where it was in 1970," a Scandinavian diplomat said recently.) It seems to be working, mainly in making things less painful for the tourist.

Another factor was thanks to the good offices of our Ker & Downey Safaris driver, a burly, smooth-talking Tanzanian named Everest. ("For the mountain," he explained, smiling: "I weighed thirteen pounds at birth and my mother named me for the biggest thing she'd heard of.") We'd had to leave Simba Kali and Colonel Austin at the border because Tanzania's entry fees for a Kenyan car and driver were still ruinous. Everest Buganga handled our passports and paperwork swiftly, then sped us south toward Arusha in a big Land Rover safari wagon. The green hills of Africa unreeled ahead of us—but Hemingway would have shuddered at the sight of them. Most were topped with ugly military radar stations, their dishes pointed towards Kenya, a reminder of the long but recently settled acrimony between these former "brothers" (with Uganda) in the so-called East African Community.

We had a lunch date at Arusha's Mount Meru Hotel with David Babu, Tanzania's director of national parks.

Amazingly, he kept it—a trim, serious man in a dark blue leisure suit. Over lunch he confirmed what we'd heard about the Serengeti's problems. "Three or four years ago," Babu said, "there were perhaps four thousand elephants in Serengeti. Now only four hundred fifty remain."

But Tanzania's largest reserve, the Selous—named for the great African hunter-naturalist Frederick Courtenay Selous—that covers some 21,000 square miles, has been hit even harder. The Selous held more than 100,000 elephants in the 1970s, but now contains fewer than 30,000. "All of the mature elephants—the big tuskers and the wise old matrons—have been killed," Babu said. "Those that remain are mere teenagers." Since elephants learn everything from herd etiquette to survival from their elders and mature at approximately the same rate as humans, the Selous teenagers are without direction. ("They're wild in the streets, as it were," a Kenyan who'd hunted there recently had told me. "These juvenile delinquents are always getting into trouble, and too often getting killed for it.")

Rhinos are in worse shape, Babu said, and Tanzania planned to transplant some of those that remain, possibly from the Selous, to Rubondo Island in Lake Victoria and the small but easily monitored Lake Manyara National Park to protect them from poachers. "We have only six hundred men in our anti-poaching units," he added, "and we need at least twice that many. We also need new weapons and more of them, we need vehicles for patrol work and road maintenance, we need more housing for parks employes, and with tourism increasing in the last two or three years, we need more beds to accommodate them. Tanzania's seventeen national parks and game reserves occupy more than twenty-five percent of the country, and we are stretched thin. We need all the help we can get."

Since we were headed south to Tarangire National Park, Babu promised to alert the warden of our impending arrival and ask him to cooperate with us fully. An amazing offer from an official of a government that only a few years ago seemed determined to make travel as miserable as possible for Westerners.

But then the Cold War is over, African nations can no longer play East and West "loyalty" games for aid money, and Tanzania desperately wants more tourism.

Not so amazingly, David Babu's message never reached Tarangire, but it wasn't necessary anyway. Senior park warden Isaac Muro, thirty-eight, and the head of his forty-five-man, anti-poaching force, Charles Mar, proved polite and cooperative nonetheless. Tarangire, located about seventy miles south of Arusha, is five hundred-twenty-five square miles of park-like game country where ancient, bulbous baobabs alternate with open bush, flat-topped acacia woodlands, grassy plains, and marshes, cut through with fast-moving brown rivers along which borassus palms stand in spike-topped clusters.

According to Muro, Tarangire's elephant population had risen from 5,000 in 1987 to some 6,200 when we were there, but they must have been hiding in the forest, because we saw only scattered groups of ten or

twenty, all of them young and well away from the roads. There are sup-
posedly five black rhinos in the park, but we spotted none of them. We
did see hartebeest, zebra, steinbok, bat-eared foxes, bateleur eagles, a very
furtive female leopard, and one evening a herd of some two hundred buffalo that stood watching and snorting as we approached to within a hundred yards. The foremost buffalo in the herd was a big, young, albino bull
who chuffed and pawed in frustration trying to make us out.

The most impressive living creatures in Tarangire, though, were the
baobabs, some of them perhaps 2,000 years old, their bulging gray trunks
gouged deep by eons of elephant tusks digging for the fibrous inner
wood that elephants chew in times of drought to get water. I've always
favored the notion that the old-time Arab slavers and elephant-poachers
were reincarnated as baobabs, to suffer centuries of goring by their erst-
while victims. Some of Tarangire's baobabs were hollow and had been
used as homes or hunting stands by the "Bushmen." We went into one
that measured about ten by fifteen feet inside. Wooden climbing pegs led
ladderlike into the hollow trunk overhead, and other pegs on the outer
bark allowed bowmen to sit on the upper branches and pick off their
prey.

"Have you noticed that you never see a young baobab?" Bill said.
"They seem to sprout full grown. Unfortunately they're getting rarer all
the time in East Africa, either undercut by thirsty elephants where the
herds are too numerous, or cleared by humans for farmland or villages."

Warden Muro, himself a baobab fancier, believes that most young
baobabs are killed by wildfires inadvertently set by tribal honey-hunters
when they attempt to smoke out bees to get at the hive. He is growing
young trees in a carefully tended plot in front of his office and has set
aside test areas in Tarangire to prove his hypothesis. The headquarters,
which the park officers share with the local Revolutionary Party,
Tanzania's only political party ("Must be nice to have the commissars
right next-door," Bill commented), underscored what David Babu had told
us about "needs." A rusting road-grader sat on flat tires out back along
with a defunct Land Rover, and the anti-poaching unit trotted out for our
inspection was nothing less than pitiful: the five men, only two in a sem-
blance of uniform and shod in everything from shoddy Chinese combat
boots to cracked patent leather loafers, carried an assortment of mis-
matched rifles—all bolt action, not automatic—in as many calibers.

I inspected a .404 Mauser that hadn't seen a lick of gun oil since World
War I. It felt very light, so I cracked the bolt.

No bullets.

"I have none," the sergeant carrying it told me, smiling disarmingly. "None of us have any ammunition just now."

A roster in the office indicated that Muro's unit had captured sixty-seven poachers in the park since 1985. I wondered how. Poachers in Tanzania, we'd been told, receive severe, non-appealable, thirty-year prison sentences with no parole. Facing that prospect, would a poacher armed with a G-3 or AK-47 come along peacefully at the request of a sport-shirted, loafer-shod game ranger carrying an empty, rusty, pre-World War II rifle?

Maybe so—but only in the game ranger's dreams.

Muro said his men had captured many snares set in the park, yet when we asked to see them, only one could be found—holding up a potted plant on the front verandah. We later learned that for ten wire snares a man can buy a cow, and that the bride price among many Tanzanian tribes is twenty or thirty head of cattle. Perhaps that's where the snares went, along with the missing bullets.

"There is no security in the future of a park ranger," Muro told us. "No *shamba*, no house for his old age." A beginning ranger earns $16 a month, or $192 a year before taxes. A ranger sergeant's annual wage is $326 and Muro himself—with a college degree in wildlife management—makes only $455.37 a year. "We must change this if we hope to get highly qualified and dedicated men into the parks and game departments," he said.

The corollary was obvious: A man with a rifle paying taxes, room, and board out of $16 a month will be very tempted to use that rifle against the very animals he's meant to protect, if doing so can earn him at least a bride price.

Greed is not the issue, but rather sheer survival.

"I was stuck in the mud last Christmas during the heavy rains, in the western Serengeti near my Grumeti River camp," Alfredo Pelizolli said. "It was night, and from my truck I could see more than a hundred flashlights working the dark, shining game. Each light seemed to have two men alongside it, one a rifleman, the other with a spear. They shot everything they could see—wildebeest, zebra, Tommy, Grant's, kongoni, topi. There are no elephants or lions left. No bushbuck. Finished."

He shook his head slowly, sadly.

"After thirty years of *Uhuru* (freedom), there is no hope for wildlife in Africa without sound management."

We were at Alfredo's new camp, still a-building, on the southwest shore of Lake Manyara. An old friend of Bill's, he had hunted professionally all through East and Central Africa, from Somalia to Tanzania and northwest into the Central African Republic. He was one of the first professional hunters to shift his locale to the southern Sudan after Kenya closed sport hunting in 1977. Driving a long-wheelbase Range Rover equipped with a refrigerator and carrying the horns and capes of the trophies his clients bagged on top, he specialized in such rare trophies as giant eland, Mrs. Gray's lechwe, tiang, and white-eared kob on the Boma Plateau. In the C.A.R. under the self-styled Emperor Bokassa, he lost an entire safari outfit to gratuitous confiscation—"lorries, safari wagons, guns, camp equipment, everything." His crew was in jail for three months before he could buy them out. No wonder the pessimism. Alfredo now runs three non-hunting tourist operations, at Grumeti and Manyara, and on Mnemba Island in the Indian Ocean near Zanzibar.

That night after supper we picked his brains on the wildlife situations around Africa.

"Southern Africa remains good," he said. "Not much poaching yet and not likely to be much, so long as sport-hunting safaris are afield to spot them and shoot if necessary, and so long as the *watu* benefit from the proceeds. Central Africa, I hear, is about finished—the C.A.R., Chad, Sudan, Zaire, God knows what's left in Angola after years of civil war and Cubans. Somalia, finished—chaos and civil war. Ethiopia, maybe something left, a few good tuskers. I don't know about West Africa, but I hear the forest elephant in Gabon are being hammered hard. East Africa—I doubt there are many elephants left in Uganda after Idi Amin and the warfare that's followed him. Kenya and Tanzania you know. But there is now at least a glimmer of hope with the Leakey appointment. He seems serious."

In Manyara we saw many small, fierce elephants while driving north under the scarp that makes the one hundred-twenty-three–square-mile park easy to patrol against poaching. Along the soda-stained shore, the morning we left, a pride of Manyara's famed tree-climbing lions—eight of them—obliged us by killing a buffalo near a place called Maji Moto (hot springs). They made a primal sight in the red dawn with flamingos and pelicans by the thousands flapping and squawking in the background while the lions, all blood to the eyes and elbows, devoured their prey. The shoreline was littered with the skulls, rib cages, and vertebrae of earlier kills. A big male with a blackish mane and olive-colored pelt tore at the buff's stomach to lap at the blood in the stomach cavity, his forelegs bulging as he ripped, veins distended. He looked up at me and our eyes met; his were flat, amber, merciless.

Sad if we lost this sight forever, I thought.

More power to his jaws and claws!

"Africa's too good for us," Bill said. "Better that we'd never been created."

"Strange, isn't it," Everest countered from behind the wheel, "how Bwana Masharubu, at least here at Manyara, seems to prefer buffalo to zebra, wildebeest, or even impala."

Bwana Masharubu, which means Mister Mustache, is the safari drivers' code name for the lion. Everest had been amusing himself during my reverie by counting skulls.

We heard more tales of rampant meat-poaching from the professional hunters at Ker & Downey's headquarters near Arusha, where we stopped on our return to the border.

"A few years back, I discovered a snare line that must have been six or eight miles long," said Harry Muller, a tough old pro who's featured in George Butler's fine pro-hunting film, *In the Blood*. "The men who tended it were living in a house made of skins as big as this verandah we're sitting on. Bone piles as high as the roofs. In the Mwezi area we chased out a poaching gang and captured eight hundred firearms: muzzle-loading nineteenth-century twelve-bore muskets. The trouble now is that the poachers are going into the roadless areas where the game is concentrated and the game scouts are afraid to go after them. What they need is expert tracking teams, like the old Selous Scouts in Zimbabwe. Bushmen like the Watidiga—those little chaps who click their tongues down at Lake Eyasi. But the Tidiga aren't interested, even if they're asked." He sipped his coffee. "We'll never see the big tuskers again, the hundred-pounders of yore—though I've seen some seventy- and eighty-pound ivory coming out of Ruaha National Park. But the elephant can be saved if government is serious. You know, Bill, I thought it was gone, I'd accepted it. Now at least there's a spark of hope."

Abdi Omar Bashir, aged forty-four, stood before a map in his office at the Langata headquarters of the Kenya Wildlife Service, his eyes flashing. A tall, trim, ruthless cop with twenty-four years of service in the paramilitary General Service Unit, he wore starched khakis pressed crisp enough to cut the throats of at least three *shifta* before losing their crease. And he'd gladly cut them.

"Our intelligence is good," Leakey's deputy director for enforcement said. "We know the routes they take from Somalia across the Tana and Galana rivers." He slashed at the map with a ruler. "They follow the oil exploration cut lines here, here, and here. I want to site ambushes along these routes. And I hope to train a good staff soon—men I know I can trust, from the G.S.U.—so I can get out in the field and oversee these operations."

When Bashir was seconded to the wildlife department last November, he found it shot through with corruption. Even low-level clerks drove Mercedes sedans, and gate guards at the national parks were skimming off half the receipts. From the early to mid-1980s, park rangers themselves were killing the rhinos and elephants in their charge, and when Somali poaching picked up in 1986, they often looked the other way in return for a share of ivory and rhino horn profits. Then Leakey threatened to fire up to a third of the department's employees (or, worse, turn them over to Bashir's ministrations). Among other sudden improvements, park receipts more than doubled within a month of Leakey's announcement.

"My first priority was to clean things up," Bashir said. "I have the authority to do so from the director and from the highest power in the land"—namely Daniel arap Moi, whose skin he'd saved during an abortive Kenya Air Force coup attempt in 1982. "I've been recruiting new game scouts from the northern tribes—Samburu, Rendille, Turkana, Wandorobo, and Borana, men who know the bush as well as the *shifta* and can live in it like you do your house." He has also been vetting captured *shifta* and "turning" some of them.

"Set a thief to catch a thief, as they say."

With his G.S.U. training cadre, Bashir initiated a "boot camp" as tough as Parris Island at Lake Magadi in the searing depths of the Rift Valley. Magadi is the world's second largest source of soda ash, after California's Salton Sea, and temperatures in the alkaline flats routinely reach one hundred-twenty windless degrees. There his new recruits undergo six weeks of tough paramilitary training in weapons, tactics, communications, and desert survival.

"Yes," Bashir said, "we need good weapons, good radios, good, fast transport on the land and in the air. But mostly we need good discipline and dedication. We've got the good men now, and we can win this war—we will win it. I promise you that this will be done."

After that, I almost enlisted on the spot. But when I tried to confirm an invitation from Bashir to visit the Magadi boot camp, he never returned my calls....

Helicopter gunships flapped home to roost at the Voi headquarters of Tsavo East National Park, their olive-drab hulls flushing rusty-pink in the sunset. They were Hughes 500s, on loan from the British Special Air Services, and they'd just returned from a day's pursuit of six *shifta* through the scrub savannah of the Tiva River country to the north. Fifty men from three of Kenya's anti-poaching units were still out, trying to cut the poachers' track. The Somalis were said to be in camouflage and armed with automatic rifles shooting the 7.62 mm NATO round—probably G-3s. We sat near a parapet of the Voi Safari Lodge, watching the clusters of elephants near the waterhole below. As at Amboseli, the elephants of Tsavo—the most heavily poached of Kenya's parks and with 8,034 square miles within its boundaries the largest—have learned to stay close to lodges. The tourists may not feed them peanuts, yet, but at least there is soldiery nearby.

A month earlier, Tsavo's game scouts had made contact with a poaching band and killed four *shifta*. Others were hit but escaped into the wasteland anyway, leaving blood trails and bloody clothing. The *shifta* are tough.

Leakey claims his men are killing ten poachers for every elephant lost since his appointment. But when we were in Kenya early in 1990, the score was sixty-six elephants killed in Tsavo alone (twenty-seven of them in January) against a "body count" of "one hundred to one hundred fifty" poachers nationwide. That is little more than two-to-one. Leakey may be falling into what's become known as the "Westmoreland Trap." Either that, or somebody's math is wrong. From the whap-whap of gunship rotors to the We-Will-Win rhetoric, it all sounded ominously familiar— echoes of Saigon in the '60s.

"These are desperate men," senior park warden Stephen M. Gichangi said of the *shifta* when we finally talked with him the following morning. "They have to kill, fight, rob to live. There is civil war in Somalia now, fierce fighting between the clans, and there are many defectors. But this is total war. We will pursue them [the Tiva River *shifta*] into Somalia if necessary. The Tiva is beyond the park's northern boundary, so we are fighting them *outside the park*, not within it any longer."

After Bashir, the speeches were getting too familiar.

Then a short, trimly built white man with a decidedly military bearing, starched green uniform and web belt, topped by a green beret that bore a silver-and-red badge in the shape of a rhinoceros, marched up to Gichangi, clicked his heels together, and snapped off a crisp, open-handed, British-style salute. This man would prove to be Patrick Hamilton, now an advisor and reconnaissance pilot for Tsavo, formerly the park's senior warden on two occasions (1981 and 1987). But he'd made the politically incorrect mistake of taking his job too seriously for that era. When the locals kept allowing their cattle into the park to graze, despite his warnings, he simply shot a few cows. That would never do. Hamilton was removed from his post. Now he was back, flying long, exhausting missions in a Super Cub, and lately a newly donated Christen A-1 Husky STOL plane, after enemies more dangerous than *ng'ombes.*

Hamilton promised to rendezvous with us in his plane later that day and point out from the air a site he'd recently discovered where the *shifta* had killed three elephants. When he climbed into his cockpit to take off, I noticed he had a G-3 assault rifle tucked away in the back seat.

Good hunting, I thought. And meant it.

As we drove to the rendezvous, we passed two groups of elephants feeding near a sluggish, forested stream. They were red-skinned from rolling in the ocherous Tsavo mud, and stayed well away from the road—flaring their ears and raising, then tucking their trunks when we approached. Very spooky. Almost enough to make one think they'd been shot at from vehicles in the not-so-distant past.

*Shifta* travel on foot, game scouts on wheels.

Hamilton's Husky rendezvoused with us that afternoon and swooped low two or three times over the thorn scrub. We pushed into the killing ground accompanied by a reserve anti-poaching unit called up from the Masai Mara for the Tiva River operation. I've described the sights, stench, and silence of what we found already, at the beginning of this story. The depression I felt on leaving that scene of slaughter was only deepened by the news that the Tiva River sweep had failed to make contact that day, and the units involved were being withdrawn. The anticlimax was numbing.

S O THE QUESTION REMAINS: What is the future of Africa's wildlife? From what we'd seen in six weeks of virtually nonstop travel through Kenya and Tanzania, it seems clear that in the short run, the glamour animals—the elephants, the predatory cats, the buffalo and perhaps the grander ungulates—can be saved in modest numbers if the policies Richard Leakey began are carried through. With the Cold War over, African governments have become aware that they must clean up their acts, cease using government office as a license to steal, and become more efficient in their use of Western aid monies. Rampant *magendo* (bribery) in black Africa has discouraged foreign investment in economies that were fragile to begin with. Ten years ago, fully fifteen Japanese firms were operating in Kenya, but only two remain today. So wildlife tourism remains the biggest foreign-currency earner in East Africa's economy, at least until such time as the area can develop industry of its own.

But wildlife tourism will draw visitors only as long as the wildlife remains. Better pay for park and wildlife employees will ensure that at least the game scouts themselves don't resume poaching. Firm, hard-nosed, incorruptible leadership like that provided by Leakey and Bashir must continue and spread to other countries.

The ivory ban has already knocked the bottom out of the world market for that substance, and that seems to be slowing the commercial poaching.

Meat-poaching is another matter. Black Africa's 517 million people are hungry and are likely to remain so. Snares are easily procured; rifles are abundant thanks to the continent's three decades of virtually nonstop wars —"The Kalashnikov Revolution," as the elephant expert Iain Douglas-Hamilton calls the proliferation of firearms in Africa.

Not until Africans develop an esthetic sense for wildlife similar to that in the West is meat-poaching likely to diminish. And a hungry belly is not easily silenced by esthetic arguments. Nor are cattle-killing predators or crop-eating wild herbivores likely to be *oooh*-ed and *aaah*-ed over in any agricultural society, let alone meat-hungry Africa, anytime soon.

Leakey's plan to fence Kenya's game parks—at a cost of $50 to $100 million—should help on that score, by keeping wildlife confined to its own spaces. The parks and reserves of the African future will, as a result, come closer and closer to resembling alfresco zoos, with air-conditioned buses traveling paved roads past fences behind which "wild" animals browse.

But why go all the way to Africa, when Busch Gardens or Lion Country Safari or Disney World is closer at hand? African wildlife, in paying its own way as Leakey demands, is likely to turn Africa into the world's largest theme park. Still, such a future is better than none at all and will at least ensure a modicum of "biodiversity" on the planet.

Busch Gardens is better than a parking lot, I guess.

The graver danger for wildlife's future, though, is human overpopulation. Everywhere we went in East Africa we saw settlements, crops, and cattle crowding right up to park edges. Black Africa's people will increase to a billion in less than twenty-five years. Famine and disease (even AIDS) are not likely to dampen that projection very significantly, according to demographers. Since I first visited Africa in 1964, whole game plains have been lost to the plow and the tin roof. As habitat declines, so too does wildlife. And as human populations soar, even more habitat will inevitably be lost, until wildlife can no longer pay its own way through tourism.

Then it will all be gone. For what government can stand against the demands of a hungry people?

The point was underscored at our last stop on the long trail. The Arabuko-Sokoke National Forest Reserve, at one hundred-forty-three square miles the largest single tract of virgin forest on the Kenya coast and one of the few remaining patches of lowland forest in East Africa, lies in the hills back of Malindi near the burgeoning resort town of Watamu. It provides rich and diverse habitat for many rare species of flora and fauna—including six threatened bird species, two of them—the Sokoke Scops owl and Clarke's weaver—found nowhere else on the planet. Little wonder that some conservationists consider it the second most important bird habitat on mainland Africa.

We spent two days in the Arabuko-Sokoke in the company of a talented birder, David Ngala, thirty-seven, who works for the Kenya Forest Service, and an old friend of Bill's, an Englishman named David Lockwood, fifty-five, who has been trying for five years to get the forest designated a sanctuary. So far to no avail, though Lockwood has spent nearly all his available money on the project.

"What with establishing a tented camp in the forest, throwing receptions and dinners for responsible officials, to which nobody came I might add, drafting proposals and having them printed again and again," Lockwood says, "I'm just about broke. Nobody cares. God, I'm tired of it!"

In Lockwood's beat-up old Land Rover, nicknamed The Battlewagon, we chugged through miles of forest on red-dirt roads and walked deep into the forest with David Ngala looking for the Sokoke Scops owl, meanwhile keeping a close lookout for snakes. The forest is home to cobras (spitting, black, and Egyptian), black and green mambas, night adders, puff adders, and gaboon vipers, as well as to rare birds and trees. Ngala knows how to imitate the owl's soft, slurred whistle, and one evening just before dark we finally struck up a conversation with a pair of them.

Walking softly, we came up to a low manilkara tree—a rare species of hardwood—and spotted them, silhouetted against the evening sky not ten or twelve feet over our heads. David whistled back and forth with them for ten minutes, the tiny, earless owlets cocking their heads as they tried to make us out. All snake fears had vanished.

"It is sweet, is it not?" David Ngala asked. His smile was luminous in the purpling gloom.

Though there are perhaps sixty to a hundred elephants in the forest's depths, we never saw them. That close to an exploding coastal population, they had long ago learned discretion. We could hear them though, rustling, breaking off branches to eat, now and then grumbling their bellies in intra-group communication, or trumpeting in alarm when we got too close. We did manage to see a rarer mammal, though—the golden-rumped elephant shrew, a snouty, five-inch-long insectivore believed to be unique to the Sokoke forest. It was moving fast across the two-track in front of The Battlewagon as we came around a blind corner, and as it disappeared into the ferns, it in effect mooned us.

Yes, it does indeed have a yellow rump.

As if in sympathetic response, the heavens pulled a disappearing act that night—a total eclipse of the full moon. Roaring back to Lockwood's seaside bungalow in Watamu in The Battlewagon, which had lost its muffler, we saw Africans sitting outside their houses on the forest's edge, awed by the sky's magic. No doubt some of them were the same men we'd seen in the forest that day, blithely felling endangered hardwoods against government orders and lugging them out on the backs of pickup trucks for sale to the Arab carvers of trinkets and builders of *dhows* up and down the coast. Though locals are allowed in the forest only to collect dead *kuni* (firewood), we'd seen at least one seven-ton Toyota lorry laden to the limits of its springs with fresh-felled cynometra logs ten inches in diameter.

Hey. It's a living.


I sat up late that night watching the eclipsing moon go dark red under the Earth's curved shadow. Thinking about East Africa's plight—indeed, all of black Africa's future. In my own lifetime I had seen this quarter of the continent go from a wild, rich gameland, a hunter's heaven, to a murderous pesthole. But could any "enlightened" ecoconscious European, Asian, or American really blame black Africans for what we'd seen? We Americans killed off our vast bison herd in only a dozen years, and are even now felling what remains of our climax forests, from coast to coast, for short-term profit. Europe was tamed long ago, most of Asia swept of all but thc rcmnants of its wildlife, and what tropical forests remain, the Japanese are dropping in a hurry.

As for the rainforests of tropical America, well....

The moon was the color of darkened blood by now, totally eclipsed. I did not wait for it to re-emerge.

Africa, *addio*.

# Glossary

*adui*—enemy, opponent, foe
*angalia*—watch out, beware, pay attention, notice
*asante*—thank you
*askari*—soldier or guard, said of both men and certain animals like the elephant and the buffalo, where younger bulls protect the old ones.

*bangi*—marijuana
*barabara*—highway, broad trail
*barafu*—ice
*baridi*—cold
*bibi*—girl, young woman
*biltong*—jerky, sun-and-wind dried meat
*'bogo*—Cape buffalo, short for *mbogo*; also called *nyati* or buff
*buibui*—a long black dress worn by Coastal women, also means "spider"
*bunduki*—gun, rifle
*bwana*—mister, sir

*chai*—tea
*chakula*—food
*choo*—latrine, toilet (pronounced "cho")
*choroa*—Beisa oryx
*chui*—leopard
*chuma*—iron
*chumvi*—salt

*damu*—blood
*dawa*—medicine; a charm or talisman provided by a witchdoctor
*debe*—metal jerrycan for carrying extra water or gasoline
*dikidiki*—the dik dik, or "Double Richard," smallest of antelopes
*donga*—a gulley, arroyo, or dry wash
*dudu*—large insect
*duka*—a shop or general store
*duma*—cheetah
*dume*—male, masculine in all senses, virile, a bull

*effendi*—sir, a military form of address

*farasi*—horse
*'faro*—rhinoceros (short for *kifaro*)
*fimbo*—stick, cane
*fisi*—hyena
*funga*—make ready, prepare, as in *Funga safari* (Make ready the journey)
*funo*—red duiker

*gambo*—far away,overseas
*gani*—what? why? as in *Habari gani?* (What news?) or *Kitu gani?* (What is it?)
*gari*—car or truck

*habari*—news,information,a report of conditions
*hapa*—here
*hapana*—no;there is none
*hatari*—danger
*heri*—happiness,good luck,success
*honga*—a bribe,also called *dash, baksheesh, or chai* (literally "tea")
*huku*—there,that place

*iko*—there is,or is there,depending on its place in a sentence
*ikweta*—the equator,a concept taught only in schools
*ini*—the liver,or the inmost seat of feeling

*jaa*—dungheap,garbage dump,also the direction "north"
*jabali*—a rocky hill or upthrust,a "jebel"in Arabicized English
*jambo*—hello (also *salamu*,from the Arabic)
*jicho*—eye
*jike*—female animal
*jini*—djinn,genie—very common along the Coast
*Juju*—Gog and Magog. Some Muslims say that on the last day of creation,Juju and Majuju
    will come and eat up all the houses and stones
*juu*—high up,overhead,on top,as in *"Panda juu,"* —"Climb up there"

*kabila*—tribe
*kabisa*—completely,utterly,thoroughly,quite
*kahawa*—coffee
*kali*—very fierce,strict,demanding,despotic
*kambi or kampi*—encampment,camp
*kanga*—guinea-fowl,also a colorful wrapping of cloth worn by townswomen
*kanzu*—a long white robe like a nightshirt
*kata*—to cut
*kikoi*—a patterned cloth wraparound skirt worn by both men and women
*karibu*—come near,approach,enter
*kiberiti*—sulphur-tipped matches
*kiboko*—hippopotamus
*kidogo*—little,small,a little bit
*kifaro*—rhinoceros
*kiu*—dry,thirsty,drought-ridden,waterless
*kloof*—South African word for a deep ravine
*kondoo*—sheep
*kongoni*—hartebeest
*korongo*—roan antelope
*kufa*—dead
*kumi*—ten
*kuru*—waterbuck
*kushoto*—to the left

*kuja*—come here
*kuku*—a chicken
*kulia*—to the right
*kwa*—by, with, at, for, in, into, on, etc.—a very important preposition
*kwaheri*—farewell, goodbye, adios, literally "with good luck"
*kwale*—francolin, spurfowl, any partridge-like bird
*kwikwi*—hiccup
*kwisha*—finished
*kwenda*—let's go, come along

*labda*—maybe, perhaps
*lakini*—but, yet, however, nevertheless
*lala*—to sleep, take a nap
*letti*—bring, fetch
*lini*—down
*loma*—badger or anteater
*lugga*—dry riverbed, ravine

*mavi*—feces, excrement, ie. "bullshit"
*maji*—water
*makende*—testicles
*mamba*—crocodile
*manamouki*—female, both human and animal
*manyatta*—a tribal village
*masharubu*—mustachios
*mawe*—rock, stone
*mayai*—eggs
*maziwa*—milk
*mbaya*—bad
*mbili*—two
*mbogo*—Cape buffalo, also *nyati* or *'bogo*
*mbuni*—ostrich
*mbuzi*—goat
*mbuzi mawe*—klipspringer, also called *ngurunguru*
*mbwa*—dog
*mbwa wa mwitu*—jackal or African hunting dog
*mchawi*—a wizard, witch doctor, practitioner of black magic
*memsaab*—lady, wife
*mguu*—leg
*mimi*—I, me
*mingi*—many
*mkono*—arm of a person, but *mkono wa ndofu* is the trunk of an elephant
*mkorofi*—evil-minded, malgnant, enraged, said of an elephant in *musth*
*mkubwa*—big
*mkuki*—spear
*mkuti*—split palm branches used for thatching
*mkutano*—meeting place
*mlango*—door, entryway
*moja*—one

*moran*—tribal warrior
*moto*—hot,fire
*motokaa*—motor car,a truck
*moyo*—heart
*mpishi*—a cook or chef
*mtoto*—baby,human or animal
*mtu*—a man
*Mungu*—God,also called *Ngai*
*mvua*—rain
*mwivi*—thief
*mzee*—a tribal elder or old man,and a term of respect
*mzigo*—butter
*mzungu*—a white man,also means something surprising,ingenious or tricky
*mzuri*—good,beautiful,excellent,fine

*na*—and,or,with
*namna*—like,sort of,similar to
*nane*—eight
*ndege*—bird,airplane
*ndio*—yes
*ndito*—young girl,virgin
*nne*—four
*ndofu*—elephant,also called *tembo*
*ndugu*—relative,brother,sister,cousin,fellow tribesman
*Ngai*—God,also called *Mungu*
*ngiri*—warthog
*ngoma*—drum,a dance
*ng'ombe*—ox,cow,cattle
*nguruma*—to make a rumbling or roaring noise,like a lion or thunder
*nguruwe*—bush-pig
*ni*—is,are
*nini*—who,what,as in *kwa nini?* (for what—ie. why?)
*njia*—road
*nugu*—monkey
*nyama*—meat or game animal
*nyamera*—topi antelope
*nyani*—baboon
*nyati*—Cape buffalo,also called *mbogo, 'bogo* or buff
*nyegere*—ratel or honey badger (a fierce customer)
*nyeusi*—black
*nyoka*—snake
*nyumba*—house,hut,dwelling,nest,lair
*nyumbu ya montu*—wildebeest

*paa*—small antelope,like an impala,blue duiker or suni
*pahala*—sable antelope,also called *mbarapi*
*paka*—domestic cat
*panga*—long,curved bush knife,like a machete
*paketi*—a packet,as of cigarettes

*pamba*—cotton
*panda*—to climb
*papa*—shark
*pembe*—horn, also the tusk of an elephant
*perere*—tree hyrax
*pesipesi*—very swiftly
*piga*—to shoot, to hit, to punch etc.
*pilipili*—pepper
*pimbi*—rock hyrax
*pofu*—eland, also called *mbunju*
*polepole*—very slowly
*pongo*—bushbuck, also called *mbawala*
*punda*—donkey
*punda milia*—zebra (you can get a laugh out of your safari crew by playing dumb and calling a zebra a *punda malaya*, which means "donkey whore.")

*radi*—thunderclap (*piga radi* is to thunder)
*rafiki*—friend
*rima*—deep pit for trapping large animals
*risasi*—cartridge, bullet
*risiti*—a receipt
*rudi*—go back, turn back
*rungu*—knob-kerri, warclub, any knobbed stick

*saba*—seven
*safi*—clean, pure, clear, bright
*safidi*—to clean up, put in order, arrange neatly
*safiri*—to travel (safari is simply a journey)
*sahani*—dish, plate
*sahib*—sir, master (used more on the Coast)
*salala*—meat from the backstraps, sirloin
*salamu*—hello (mainly on the Coast), also *jambo*
*samaki*—any fish
*sambamba*—side by side, in line, alongside
*sana*—very much, in a high degree, as in *kubwa sana* (very big)
*sasa*—right now, immediately
*sawasawa*—alike, equally, just the same
*shabaha*—gunsight; a target; the act of aiming
*shaitani*—the devil (also *shetani*)—he's very much alive in East Africa
*shamba*—a farm, garden, plantation, country estate etc.
*shamiri*—to load a gun
*shanta*—backpack, haversack, rucksack
*shauri*—a plan, affair, design or intention, as in the fatalistic watchword of Swahili-speaking Africa, *Shauri ya Mungu*,—It is the will of God—or, It's his *shauri*, don't get involved in it.
*shemali*—the left hand, the north, the north wind
*shenzi*—barbarous, uncivilized, uncouth, said often of Wandorobos and some white men.
*shilingi*—shilling (the common currency in Kenya, Tanzania and Uganda)
*shimo*—pit, hole, excavation

*shonde*—cowdung, dried patties of which are often used for fuel
*shufti*—look-see, reconnaissance
*shuka*—a piece of cloth about two meters long, worn as a toga or loincloth
*siafu*—small, fierce, brownish-red driver ants that attack all living things
*siagi*—butter
*sigareti*—cigar or cigarette
*silaha*—weapon, armament, as in *Silaha ya Mungu*, Weapon of God (lightning)
*simama*—to stop, stay where you are, remain immobile
*simba*—lion. A lioness is a *simba jike*, a male *simba dume*.
*sime*—a short, double-edged sword, broader near the point.
*sita*—six
*sokwe*—chimpanzee
*songololo*—a gigantic black-and-red poisonous millipede of the Coast, also called *chungalo-lo*, Tanganyika Train or Mombasa Bus
*sufuria*—metal cookpot, sometimes large enough to boil a missionary
*sumu*—poison, often made from the pulped and boiled bark of the acocanthera plant and smeared on arrowhead or spears.
*swala granti*—Grant's gazelle
*swala tomi*—Thomson's gazelle
*swala twiga*—gerenuk (literally "gazelle giraffe")
*swila*—the spitting cobra

*takataka*—filth, junk, garbage, worthless stuff
*tamu*—sweet, nice, enjoyable
*tandala kubwa*—greater kudu
*tandala ndogo* or *kidogo*—lesser kudu
*tano*—five
*tatu*—three
*taya*—oribi antelope
*tayari*—ready, at hand, prepared
*tembea*—take a walk, stroll
*tembo*—elephant, also *ndovu*
*tia*—put in, insert (as ammunition)
*tisa*—nine
*toa*—take out, unload (as ammunition)
*tohe*—reedbuck
*tumbako*—tobacco, usually of the chewing or snuff variety
*tumbo*—belly, stomach
*tumbua*—disembowel, gralloch
*twiga*—giraffe

*uhuru*—freedom, independence
*ujamaa*—brotherhood, kinship
*ujamu*—a piece of rope passed through the nose of an ox
*ujuba*—violence, tyranny, oppression
*ukuba*—bad smell, misfortune, a curse

*wadi*—seasonal watercourse, ravine

*walakini*—however, but
*wapi*—where
*wewe*—you (singular)—plural is *ninyi*

*yake*—his, hers, its
*yako*—yours
*yangu*—my, mine
*yupi*—who

*zaka*—a quiver for arrows
*zamani*—time gone by, the old days, a period, era or epoch
*zariba*—wall of thornbrush built around a camp or village to keep out lions, etc., more
   properly called a *boma*

(Author's note: Most of these common safari terms are in Kiswahili, the *lingua franca* of East Africa, which is largely Bantu in origin with a hefty dose of Arabic and a touch of English added for flavor. It's a charming language, simple, strong, euphonious, lending itself to wit, aphorism and a kind of tough, fatalistic eloquence. Once you've heard it spoken on safari and absorbed a few words, you'll never forget it—just as you'll never forget the stark beauty of Africa and its people. Sometimes in the depths of a long, cold, northern winter night, I dream in Kiswahili. *Kwaheri!*)